I0409825

# Through Brown Eyes

## A Short History of the
Dallas Brown Berets
Organization
and the Chicano Movement
from my Point of View

Juan M. Pérez
**Prime Minister**
of the
Dallas Brown Berets

1980

*Through Brown Eyes*

Copyright © 2015 by Rev. Juan M. Pérez. All rights reserved.

No part of this publication may be reproduced, stored in a retrieval system or transmitted in any way by any means, electronic, mechanical, photocopy, recording or otherwise without the prior permission of the author except as provided by USA copyright law.

Book design copyright © 2014 by Rev. Juan M. Pérez, LLC. All rights reserved.
Cover design by Rev. Juan M. Pérez
Interior design by Rev. Juan M. Pérez

Published in the United States of America

ISBN-13: 978-1537156446
ISBN-10: 1537156446

1. Nonfiction / History / Contemporary Political
2. Nonfiction / Social Science / Ethnic Studies

# Index

**POESIA DEL SOL**
(Poetry of the Sun)
Placed throughout the book

# THROUGH BROWN EYES

## PREFACE

The "gentleman" on the cover is who I **_used_** to be. I wrote the contents of this book over thirty years ago. At the time I had a completely different worldview from today. From one point of view you could say I grew up (matured). On the other hand, I did not have the desired results from my involvement in the Chicano Movement. It was a dream on the one hand (Aztlan, that is), and on the other, when I most needed help in my life due to many bad decisions and a terrible addiction to cocaine, and about to lose my marriage to divorce, I found no help from the Movement. I was disillusioned and walked away.

I left the contents of the earlier manuscript pretty much as I wrote it at the time. I made some grammar corrections, fixed some typos, and added minor notes in some places. There were some things I did not "fix" because I felt it would have changed the intent I had at the time. I may not see eye to eye, with the Juan Pérez of the Brown Berets, but I still have great respect for his commitment to a cause, his determination to be faithful to the struggle, and for his endeavor to write this manuscript which never got published in his time. I know he (that is I at the time, of course) truly wanted to publish this book. He needed the money. I who was he, but am no longer that man, but me today, a changed man, I will do it for him.

# THROUGH BROWN EYES

Editing this manuscript was a trip to the past for me. I guess you could say that this is the only way I will ever travel through time backwards. I hope you find much of interest in these pages, as we look at the world through the eyes of Brown Beret Juan M. Pérez, a Chicano point of view, "Through Brown Eyes."

Please understand that I may not agree with any or all of the contents of this book. I should not be held accountable for what a 28 year old version of myself said all those many years ago. He was he, and I am me. If anyone wants to know what I believe today, then get in touch with me and ask me at:

http://www.PracticalCounseling.Com.

The following are "his" words, **_not_** mine.

# THROUGH BROWN EYES

## UNAS PALABRAS

The compilation of this book took me four years of active collecting, considerable reviewing, editing and preparation. Actually, though, I started collecting this information since the first day I walked into the Dallas Brown Berets' "Headquarters" in 1970 and was handed a leaflet containing information on the Organization and a brown beret (cap). I still have the beret and you will find the leaflet in the contents of this book.

My reasons for preparing this book include:

(I) As Public Relations Coordinator of the Dallas Chapter, my primary function is "to expose as much about the Organization, in as positive a manner as possible, so as to perpetrate an image that is truly representative of the attitudes, beliefs, philosophy, and motivation of the Brown Berets."

(2) I believe that past, and in many cases present, information on the activities of the Brown Berets have been largely characterized as negative. This is true in many of the cases I have included in this book. The reader will notice the difference in the facts I present and some of the allegations and misrepresentations inferred by reporters in many of the newspaper articles I included in this book. I intend for the material in this book to be as factual and complete as possible. Sources include the files of the Dallas

---

Chapter as well as others of Los Brown Berets de Tejas, Aztlan Organization; many community, as well as metropolitan newspapers from throughout the Southwest; memories of many members of the Organization (including myself); and documents obtained from intelligence sources through the Freedom of Information Act/Privacy Act (FOIA/PA), such as FBI documents on the Brown Berets.

(3) I believe there are many individuals who have had or still have questions on the Brown Berets and want to know the answers. And even though I don't tell "all", I have included more details on most of the Organization's public activities than any other source (except another Beret member) possibly could.

(4) I owe it to La Raza to publish facts on an Organization which has played, and will continue to play, such an integral part of the Chicano Movement, the Chicano Community, as well as the Struggle for the Liberation of Aztlan. I owe much to several persons, in reference to the preparation of this book.

Also very important was John Fullenwider of the Bois d'Arc Patriots. His assistance helped me to improve the quality of the information in this book greatly. John is an individual with unlimited potential and self-motivation. These qualities make him one of the most valuable assets of the Bois d'Arc Patriots. GRACIAS John. Another individual who also assisted is W. Addison Durboraw. At the time of this writing, Addison is the host of a Brown Beret produced television program "IN OUR OPINION," in Dallas, Texas. He is also the author of short stories and articles on various subjects.

In addition, let me clarify some points.

---

# THROUGH BROWN EYES

In the chapters where I detail activities or incidents, I put these in chronological order. I have included as much material as I felt necessary to get the message or point across for each instance.

Some of the information which I included in its entirety, especially articles from newspapers and documents of intelligence agencies, were not always clear or had words misspelled. I typed the information just as it was in the source, but I either clarified it or spelled it correctly by using insertions like this ( - JMP).

I do concede that this book does not contain everything about the Brown berets. There is information Los Brown Berets de Tejas, Aztlan Organization choose not to make public. Some of the information the Organization chooses to exclude from this book is that which concerns the internal structure and/or procedures and functions of the Brown Berets. Other information could be used by enemies of the Organization and/or La Raza to the disadvantage of El Movimiento. C/S. Juan M. Pérez

Hence the following:

# THROUGH BROWN EYES

## Chapter One
## *LAS BOINAS CAFE*

**THE VANGUARD**

*"No longer will we whisper a just cause; we will shout it out in hopes that it will reach receptive ears; our hunger for freedom can only be quelled with justice and liberty" - National Brown Berets.*

WHO ARE THE BROWN BERETS?

From 1967 to 1972 more than 5,000 Chicanos joined the National Brown Berets. Founded by David Sanchez, the national organization has members throughout Aztlan -- in California, where the Organization was born, Arizona, Nuevo Mejico, Tejas, and Colorado in the Southwest and in other U.S. cities.

Uniforms vary depending on what part of the country or what city a member is from. Generally, combat boots, khaki pants, bush jacket, and the ever present brown beret.

The Brown Berets are united by the belief in NATIONALISM and ETHNOCENTRICSM; uniting their people and their culture. They also believe in the philosophy of self-determination over their own lives, control of their own communities and great love and respect for La Raza.

# THROUGH BROWN EYES

In late 1972 the National Brown Berets released the following declaration:

Start ---

"DECLARATION FOR LA RAZA NUEVA"

The masses of LA RAZA NUEVA will no longer kneel before the emotionless White myth begging for crumbs from an exploiting system, but will reclaim their rights and their rightful place in the sun by whatever power necessary. Whatever price human dignity demands, we are ready to pay for it.

The masses of LA RAZA NUEVA have no need for outside influences to take up the struggle on all levels against the pale vampires that grow wealthy on the blood, sweat, and the misery of our people.

The masses of LA RAZA NUEVA have found a voice of their own in papers such as

# THROUGH BROWN EYES

LA RAZA, CHICANO STUDENT MOVEMENT and others of the Chicano Press Association.

The masses of LA RAZA NUEVA have "la causa es la verdad," a cause based on truth, reason and justice.

The masses of LA RAZA NUEVA have no need of a gestapo-like police arm to insure our just ideals and goals. We have something stronger and that is growing solidly among our own that will not die.

LA RAZA NUEVA has the urban worker who has grown tired of filling with money the endless pockets of industrial leeches. Sweaty foreheads and tired bodies have thundered YA BASTA!

LA RAZA NUEVA has the CAMPESINO, THE FARMWORKER, for too long enslaved by the latifundios of the United States. They have broken the chains that enslave them and are organizing to do battle for human dignity. Their life is the land for which the Joaquin Murietas, the Manos Negras, and the valientes of the Southwest fought and died for.

LA RAZA NUEVA has the Chicano student who has learned the art of surviving in a "White racist society" without losing his corazon. The Chicano Students are carving a new page in our history, making it, despite the system.

HERMANOS ESTUDIANTES, HERMANOS OBREROS, HERMANOS CAMPESINOS, HERMANOS TRABAJADORES, HERMANOS DEL PUEBLO, ORGANISENSE! Our struggle will be a long one, but the final victory will be ours!

Our struggle lies not in one leader, but in a strong people united and dedicated. Among us there are many Cesar Chavezes. Among us there are many Sal Castros. Among us there are many

---

Rudolfo "Corky" Gonzaleses. Among us there are many Luis Valdezes. Among us there are many Reies Lopez Tijerinas. Among us there are many David Sanchez. Among us there are many Joaquin Murietas. Every one of us has an obligation ...no... a duty to be as a missionary to our people wherever we go; in class, on the job, to the cantinas, to the club meetings, to your family, and to the barrios. We are all potential organizers. Remember that the Chicano who loves only himself does not really love his people.

The struggle continues and will continue hasta la victoria.

HERMANOS DO YOUR DUTY"

End ------

Also for your review I have included the "Brown Beret National Policies 1972"

Start ---

Let it be known to the universe: That these are the policies of the Brown Beret National Organization and; any person who poses to be a Brown Beret and does not follow these policies and principals is not a Brown Beret and should not be respected as one.

For too long individuals have prostituted the good name of the Brown Beret National Organization for their own self advancement, or they have prostituted the Brown Beret name for other movements. And to prevent further foreign agent insurgency; these policies have been created.

Article I

"Let it be recognized that the Brown Beret National Organization is an organization that relates its energies to the

---

historical and geographical situation the Chicano people are within.

"The situation the Chicano people are within is Geographical because the land was stolen from the Chicano people, and is national because the Chicano people are a nation of combined abilities, both survival and cultural, of which were are a nation.

"1.5 million Chicanos are also within a Sociological situation, where there is definite discrimination against Chicanos throughout the country. Whereas, wherever a Chicano is discriminated against and no matter where it may be, it is our cause to secure Human Rights as well as Civil Rights for all Chicanos.

"The existing situation has not only left a people who has lost their land, but also the destruction of our people has taken place which is a detriment to culture, heritage, and existence of La Raza.

"And because of the existing situation, we have created policies to not only create definite strategy, but also to prevent any threat to the coming nation. Whereas, we will halt any type of foreign intervention, by all means necessary.

"Article II

"History

"Let it be known to all, that the present invasion and occupation of the Southwest was not by treaty, annexation, or purchase, as we have been told by the Treaty of Guadalupe Hidalgo of 1848. But, let it be known for historical record that in 1848, Brigadier General Stephen Kearney, along with other U.S. forces, took possession of the Southwest by force.

"To prevent further battles between Anglo and Mexican gangs who fought against the occupation, at that time a treaty was resolved in 1848, which guaranteed rights to those who remained in the Southwest. And this same treaty of Guadalupe Hidalgo was violated when Ruben Salazar was not given the right to free assembly on August 29, 1970.

"The treaty was broken, and two years before 1848, the land 'was stolen with malicious evil intent, and malice. We have suffered, and we will never be free until the land is free from Anglo progress, which has been a detriment to the land, air, and water, as well as to our health.

"Because the Purchase Negotiations and Annexation took place two years after the takeover of the Southwest by U.S. forces, we declare the Treaty of Guadalupe Hidalgo invalid as well as its borders and promises.

"We also declare the invasion of the Southwest a mistake, and a historical fraud which calls for attention. Because the invasion of the Southwest was a gamble, of which, we call no dice, or misdeal, whereas, we will do all in our power to prove this historical mistake, because in history, the land always returns to the true inhabitants of that land.

"Article III

"We are Chicanos——

"We do not recognize any party which is affiliated with perpetuating, White History. Left Wing, Right Wing, Socialists, Democrats and other Foreign Ideologies have attempted to prostitute the Chicano Movement for the purpose of perpetuating Foreign Movements. We are neither Left Wing, nor Right Wing. We are Chicanos, and we denounce all White Foreigners who try to put any other label on us, in order to create LA VIDA NUEVA DE LA RAZA.

"Article IV

"Defense against Foreign Movements

"One side of the world is out to destroy the other side. The two great opposing ideologies both solicit nuclear destruction. The whole world is sucked into sick symptoms. And we wish to have no part in Foreign Movements. And we will do everything in our power to prevent foreign agent persuasion.

"We are against insurgency by communists, or republican parties or any other foreign, we are against.

"Article V

"Expression

"Small scattered incidents and mobism in the past has led to lack of organization, turmoil, and some Chicano deaths. Perhaps, at that time, there was no way to control massive demonstration by La Raza, from which we have already suffered at the hands of out-of-control police demonstrations that have only led to suffering on part of the RAZA.

"Because of this, we wish to demonstrate in an orderly organized fashion with an organized disciplined body of people who can demonstrate an expression without the problems of out-of-control mob violence.

"We are moving to show that we are right, and to illustrate to all that anger and frustration can be directed towards constructive change, and we will sacrifice our personal freedoms for significance, and to display how far we will go to make change by the usage of the right expression; whether that expression be military, or otherwise. We have the right by peaceful means to show discontent toward Local Government by the usage of free expression.

"Article VI

"Preparations

"We must prepare for the escalation of massive coordination on a national scale, rather than on a local scale, of which the development of academies is necessary in order for qualified officers to come about.

"All energies and resources must be directed toward preparations.

"All education must be directed toward channeling students into a more skilled, technical, and qualified organization of the Brown Beret National Organization.

"We must also make shelter and survival possible for Chicanos in case of disaster or evacuation. Fallout shelters as well.

"Article VII

"Absolute Militarism

"In order to create massive organization within a society, and for that organization to control the conditions around it, and in order to survive conditions, it will take sacrifice of our personal freedoms for absolute militarism, which is the fastest and strongest way to Chicano Power.

"And in order to create real power for the people for the people, Discipline is necessary.

"We must understand that discipline is necessary in order to secure orderly action which alone can triumph over the seemingly impossible conditions of confrontation against any opposing force,

"We must be able to recognize and face fear, because fear is the enemy of Discipline. Fear unchecked will lead to panic, and a unit which panics is no longer a disciplined unit but a mob.

"Absolute Militarism is needed to prevent out of control mob panic, and is also for the purpose of massive coordination.

"Article VIII

"Strategy

"By strategy, we are creating a movement by design to advance the Chicano Movement, five to ten years ahead of its time.

"La Caravana De La Reconquista is a tour and caravan of the Southwest which is becoming a continuous migrating mass of people, and this continuous migration will revolve without end. And during its travels, officers will be trained on this Academy on Wheels which will eventually change the migration track La Raza to migrate to the country and places for better living.

"Also from these studies of travel, different perimeters of safer areas will be drawn.

"Another tactic of reclamation of lands will begin, first by control of Geographical areas for a greater lead way to a greater movement, which, will take place not by force, but rather by forms of occupation.

"Further strategy, also calls for the development of more chapters who will support the front line of La Caravana De La Recoquista along with gathering resources from chapters to enforce and support special national projects of the Brown Beret National Organization.

"Article IX

"Customs

"We are a nation with a definite culture and with a land that has been stolen. We are a state of carnalismo, we are not internationalist, we are nationalist. And those who come, or live in Chicano land, must live and do as the Chicanos do.

"Article X

"Chapters

"The chapters' first job is to instruct and to follow Brown Beret National Policy of 1972.

"The job of the chapter is one of community service, or it is one of social action for change, or both.

"Another job of the local chapter is to educate the Raza about these policies as well as getting the community involved with strategies of the Brown Beret National Organization.

"Every Brown Beret Chapter is a local reserve Organization.

"It is also very important that each chapter understand that it is in itself a support office to reinforce the Brown Beret National Organization strategies with funds, reinforcements, and resources for greater national coordination.

"Article XI

"Stop to all immediate Foreign Insurgency

# THROUGH BROWN EYES

"We are a National Organization and anyone who has associated himself with any international agency, organization, or other country is automatically terminated.

"Anyone who does not depict and practice the Brown Beret National Policy 1972, is hereby terminated.

"Any Brown Beret who is associated with the republicans, or Anglo controlled Communist Party U.S.A. or is associated with Communist Party International is hereby terminated. Any Brown Beret who identifies as being part of the small scattered incidents of the C.L.F. is terminated because they do not have the knowledge of preparations.

"Article XII

"Backers

"Despite age, profession, or income. It is of most importance that all Chicanos back each other in order to raise each other up, so that some Chicanos can have more resources for the purpose of channeling assistance to the Chicano Movement.

"It is also very important that all Chicanos working in agencies along with all Chicano Professionals use their position as a vehicle to assist the Chicano Movement.

"As well as backing each other up to raise up other Chicanos with positions, and to back each other up for support, in case anyone runs into any problems for using his position to assist the Movement.

"Article XIII

"Neutrality

"We are a neutral state, because for the world we have something to offer.

"Article XIV

"We Declare a Nation.

"We the Chicano People of the Southwest, hereby declare ourselves a nation, and a nation that has been the subject of a profit-making invasion. We are a nation with a land that has been temporarily occupied.

"And a nation with the ability to survive. We are a nation with great natural culturability. We are a nation, we who come from different ways, combing ourselves of our nation.

"We are, the good people who return nature back to its natural balance, and who bring justice to the universe.

"Article XV

"Chicano and Indian

"Even though, the Indian nation is somewhat unaware of the Chicano, as being a people who all hold more than half (in proportion to all people of Mexican decent) Indian Blood, We are of Indian-Mestizo decent, and we are of one Indian Nation with similar and related cultures before the Invasion of the primitive white man.

"As far as all boundaries within the Southwest which was once Mexico, we combine all people of Indian decent as being ONE, as well as its borders, boundaries, and perimeters of the Southwest.

"Article XVI

"Further Policies

"Part A - OFFICIAL

"I.) Anyone who states: That he, or she, is a Brown Beret and does not conduct himself with real discipline is not a Brown Beret.

"2.) Anyone who states: That he, or she, is a Brown Beret and does not have Loyalty that is responsive to orders as well as ultimate respect towards the Prime-Minister Office, is not a Brown Beret.

"3.) Anyone who states: That he, or she, is a Brown Beret and does not have Loyalty to the National Ministers Office, is not a Brown Beret.

"4.) Anyone who does not accept the Prime-Minister Office as Executive Chief of the Brown Beret National Forces, is not a Brown Beret.

"Part B

"Brown Beret National Policy is to create unity within our own Barrios without the alienation of our own people. We are Chicanos in a struggle for our rights and the eventual return of our land.

"Anyone who attempts to apply any other label upon us, is in violation of National Policy. The Brown Beret National Organization is based upon years of created organization capital, and anyone who causes a threat to the Foundation is in violation of National Policy.

"Anyone who causes dissent by traveling from one chapter to another to cause disunity, among or between any chapters is in violation of National Policy.

"The Brown Beret National Organization is based upon any funds that can be gathered for communications, transportation, demonstrations, and Legal Defense.

Anyone who receives funds on other materials for the Organization, and does not turn in said funds or materials for the Organization, is in violation of National Policy.

"Part C

"All violators of National Policy are subject to disciplinary action. Rank is for coordination, and those who do not respect rank (which was coordinated for the purpose of massive action) are in violation of National Policy.

"During any event or action where there is no leadership in a community emergency situation a Beret who does not attempt to take the burden of the emergency situation, is in violation of National Policy.

"Any unit or chapter who titles themselves, or claims affiliation with, the term "Brown Beret" but does not actually affiliate with a registered chapter or unit, is in violation of National Policy.

"Any person who states that he or she in a "Brown Beret" and who is not actually affiliated with a registered chapter or unit, is in violation of National Policy.

"Any person who mistreats a soldado by applying more stress and anger than is excessive to accomplish duties, is in violation of National Policy."

End ---

Today, the Brown Berets (while still ethnocentric) are a Chicano, activist, community-oriented organization. Instead of being strictly Nationalists, the Berets are fast becoming Internationalists, in solidarity with all oppressed peoples, in the world-wide struggle against.

# THROUGH BROWN EYES

---

IMPERIALISM.

In Tejas the TEJAS Brown Berets Organization was formed in 1975. Chapters throughout Texas joined in a Confederation.

Initially, the purpose of the Confederation was to establish state-wide communication and to organize systems which would be complimentary to all chapters represented.

Today the Berets are more tightly organized under a State Board of Direction, State Manifesto and By-laws.

Each individual Chapter has its own guidelines as well as the State Guidelines. All Chapters have autonomy in all matters except those which might conflict with the State By-laws. Also, the internal structure of each Chapter may be different.

Qualifications to join the membership include: I.) The State calls for all members to be Chicano; 2.) Full dedication to the policies and Manifesto of the Organization; 3.) Local Chapters have, and take advantage of, the option to add additional qualifications.

The size of the Organization varies. In the Valley (South Tejas) there are many small chapters in many small towns (i.e. McAllen, Pharr, San Juan, etc.). The larger Chapters are from cities with larger Raza populations (Austin, Dallas, Lubbock, San Antonio, etc.). The Organization also decided that revealing the number of the membership in either the local or state contexts would serve no useful purpose to the Berets and that it could prove to their disadvantage, so said number is not to be disclosed.

Locally (Dallas, Tejas), the group was organized by Richard Medrano (the first Dallas Prime Minister) in 1969. Like the National Brown Berets, the local chapter also adopted the para-military internal structure. The Prime Minister is the person in control of the

---

whole outfit. Then there is the Vice-Minister, the Minister of Education, the Minister of Treasury, and the Minister of Intelligence. The chapter's functions were also different from today's Organization. Back then, the Dallas group limited its functions to solely political matters (i.e. supporting and/or attacking political office candidates). The group distributed Medrano literature such as bumper stickers, posters and such.

Today, the Brown Beret Organization clearly defines its objectives, its issues, its services, its policies, and its regulations.

Among the short term objectives, the Berets list: 1) to identify problems that plague the Chicano community; 2) to expose those problems; and 3) to assist the victims of those problems. Long range objectives include: the unending struggle against Imperialism and racism. And, the main objective is the liberation of Aztlan and self-determination for the Chicano peoples.

The issues include: l) Police Abuse of Authority; 2) Dual Standards of the Judicial System; 3) whatever other issue the Chicano community feels is necessary.

The services are provided for any victim (regardless of race) of an identified problem. From actual involvement to referrals, the Berets are working on a one-to-one basis.

The policies and regulations show clearly what will be expected of any new member by the Organization.

The public positions (offices) of the Brown Berets are the Public Relations Coordinator, Security Coordinator, and 1st and 2nd Assistant Directors. Besides these, the organization has decided that the rank of members and other offices need not be made public.

# THROUGH BROWN EYES

Membership throughout Aztlan (the Southwest: TEJAS, NUEVO MEXICO, ARIZONA, COLORADO, AND CALIFORNIA) is very diverse. It includes: women, men, older people, young people, college graduates, school drop-outs, Vietnam veterans, organizers, laborers, employed, unemployed, and many others.

Common characteristics in all these people include: a strong determination to meet the injustices "head on" and defeat them; to gain the liberation of the Chicano and native people; and establish Aztlan.

A portion of the State Manifesto of the Los Brown Berets de Tejas, Aztlan, gives the following statements:

"I am a Brown Beret. I will study and practice to learn our ideas. I am a student and teacher of Nationalism. I will demonstrate patience and respect in the political-learning process of nuestra Raza. I am a soldado of the nation known to Chicanos in the Southwest portion of the U.S. as Aztlan. It is for this nation (Aztlan) that I will live, fight and die for. My beret represents unity and Nationalism, the cross rifles represent my determination for land and liberation.

My goal is self-determination for the nation of Aztlan. I am against self-profit and/or self-political gain through our movement. I am part of the vanguard and offensive for the community and Aztlan. I must therefore study the enemy and learn to fight on all levels necessary, including armed struggle (as a final alternative). I will learn and teach all that I can about nuestra Cultura and historia. I will teach my children to follow the movement for liberation of nuestra Raza. I believe that capitalism and imperialism are the oppressive means of colonialization we live under. There are no privileged Brown Berets. Rank is for responsibility and capacity, not for mere authority. I must criticize those who do not meet their leadership responsibilities; but my responsibility is to support and strengthen our movement. I will be honest with the Brown Berets Organization and will resign if I cannot support their beliefs.

## LOS BROWN BERETS

Los Brown Berets Estamos Aquí,
Y Por Siempre Vamos Existir,
Por La Causa Estamos Peleando,
Y Por La Causa Vamos A Morir.

A Los Chicanos Que Somos Nosotros,
Los Derechos Nos Quieren Quitar,
Y Los Modos Que Tenemos, Y Nuestra Lengua
Nos Quieren Cambiar

Los Brown Berets Eso Peleamos,
Chicano Power Queremos Tener,
Puro Poder Para Nuestra Gente,
Poder Chicano Que Vamos Tener.

Los Brown Berets Estamos Aquí,
Y Por Siempre Vamos Existir
Por La Causa Estamos Peleando,
Y Por La Causa Vamos A Morir.

- Juan M. Pérez

# THROUGH BROWN EYES

# THROUGH BROWN EYES

---

### *Chapter Two*
### *BROWN BERETS NATIONAL ORGANIZATION*

Early Brown Beret history is full of "growing pains", events that occurred that helped shape the future of the Organization. For example, the Brown Berets were initially intended as a "militant" (as defined in the American Heritage Dictionary, 1972, page M8, "aggressive", esp. in the service of some cause.), para-military organization. The Berets at present are an "activist" (as defined in above dictionary) organization. The progression of events, in and through Brown Beret history, led to the change in the image the Organization saw in itself. The following events should give an idea to the reader of the direction the Organization in Los Angeles, California, chose to follow:

1967

In June of this year, the Young Chicanos for Community Action (Y. C. C. A.) is founded by David Sanchez and Ralph Ramirez.

On August I, Police Chief Thomas Reddin meets with community groups in Lincoln Heights, a near riot develops.

Y.C.C.A. opens the Piranya Coffee House, on October the 6th, for the purposes of community awareness and recruitment for action.

Because of constant police brutality cases, Y.C.C.A. is the first to picket the East Los Angeles Sheriff's Station and the Los Angeles Police Department's Hollenbeck Division in November.

---

# THROUGH BROWN EYES

In December the Y.C.C.A. adopted the brown beret as part of the uniform, becoming the Brown Berets.

1968

The East Los Angeles Sheriff's Department launches an all-out attempt to close the Piranya Coffee House, in January, by extensive raids and harassment of members. In February, the East Los Angeles Sheriff's Department declares Whittier Blvd. a traffic hazard and closes the street, which is mostly used by Chicanos. Brown Berets hold demonstrations on Whittier Blvd. and La Verne, on February 20th, protesting the Sheriff's Department's unjust roadblocks. Police break up demonstration of 150 with shotgun buds and arrest David Sanchez and Cruz Olmeda for disturbing the peace. Sanchez is sent to Wayside Maximum Security, where he wrote The Birth of a New Symbol, the Brown Beret manual.

On March 5, the Brown Berets and the United Mexican American Students (U.M.A.S.) helped organize walkouts at many schools including Garfield, Belmont, Roosevelt, and Lincoln High Schools, to protest discrimination against Chicanos by the educational system of Los Angeles.

Open City, an underground newspaper, estimated that 5,000 students had walked out on the first day of the walkout. This number quickly rose to 10,000 by the peak of the event. On March 8, at least 1,500 "East Los" students meet at Hazard Park and present their demands to Board of Education members. On March 5, Approximately 200 Chicano students walked out of Lincoln High School, 450 South Pickett Street, Los Angeles, at about 11:30 am. These students had presented numerous grievances to school administrators, including the removal of the fence around the school, elimination of a dress code for women, covering eating areas, removal of old facilities, and installation of a swimming pool and a juke box in the recreation areas.

# *THROUGH BROWN EYES*

Students at Roosevelt High School left that school in support of the Lincoln students. Approximately 1,000 students were in the street near Roosevelt at one time.

At about 1:00 pm, and about four blocks from Roosevelt, students began throwing rocks at police units in that vicinity. Shortly after that, a tactical alert was called by the Hollenbeck Division and other metropolitan divisions of the Los Angeles Police Department.

Some of the Lincoln High students marched to Roosevelt, and another 250 marched to the Regional Office of the Los Angeles City Board of Education, 1550 Norfolk Avenue, and presented concerns similar to those mentioned above.

Shortly after noon, students at Roosevelt began leaving classes and protesting in the area at which the Command Post was established. Some violence broke out and rocks and bottles were thrown at the police, who set about at dispersing the students from the area.

# THROUGH BROWN EYES

Damages in the incident at Roosevelt included: the windshield broken on one police unit, seven feet of wire fence in the school broken down, the automatic sprinkler system set off, two fires set in trash cans, and one officer was injured, receiving cuts under his left eye from a thrown bottle, which required hospitalization.

Another incident involving a walkout, which also occurred on March 5th, occurred at Garfield High School, 5105 East Sixth Street, in LA, when about 150 Chicano students presented a list of concerns to the school administration, including demands for better food, new buildings, new library books, elimination of all fencing, elimination of a dress code, and a demand to be treated as adults. The school Principal agreed to review the concerns and call an assembly to discuss those concerns.

At 8:50 am, on March 06, 200 Garfield High School Students walked to Atlantic Park at Sixth and Woods Streets. The group was almost entirely made up of Chicano students. At about 9:10 am, the students were addressed by Phil Castrulita and Carlos Munoz, both representatives of United Mexican American Students, and

students at California State College. Mike De La Pena of the Mexican American Student Association, also spoke.

These individuals told the high school students that they had every right to protest but that their protests should be lawful, and that they should present their demands to the Principal at Garfield High in a legal fashion. At 10:00 am the students proceeded to the Principal's office and issued a list of concerns similar to those made by the students at Lincoln High.

Also on March 06, at Jefferson High School, 1319 East 41st Street, in LA, a predominantly Black school, about 300 students gathered at the school football field and refused to attend classes. The student body President met with the students and asked them to return to classes. The protestors attended one class and again met at the school library to discuss grievances.

Local newspaper and television coverage on March 6th, blamed some of the unrest at Chicano school on "outsiders known as the Brown Berets."

On March 10, a group of Brown Berets held a meeting at Banning Park, corner of Pacific Coast Highway and Eubank Ave, one-half block from Banning High School. The Berets reportedly contacted local student leaders, gave a speech concerning student disadvantages and grievances. Literature listing the grievances was passed out urging the students to walk out of Banning High at 12:30 pm, on March ll.

On the 11th, during the walkout, the back gate of the school was locked and teachers and faculty physically barred students from leaving by the front entrance. The police brought two "Chicano community leaders" to the school. They spoke to the students and calmed them down. '

# THROUGH BROWN EYES

Three individuals were arrested for "loitering near a public school." They included two members of the Brown Berets and a "local contact" of the Organization.

On March 12, the Los Angeles Times reported in a page I-1 article that the Board of Education had agreed at a March 11 meeting to a number of student demands in an attempt to end the boycott of classes by students and teachers (some teachers refused to attend due to "unsafe conditions stemming from the walkouts"). The Board agreed to hold a special meeting at Lincoln High to discuss problems of the school in the East Los Angeles area. The Board indicated it would give amnesty to students who had boycotted their classes since March 06, but refused to remove the police from the campuses or to release students who were arrested during the demonstrations.

The Piranya Coffee House is closed down on March ill by the East Los Angeles Sheriff's Department.

On April 23, David Sanchez and Cruz Olmeda, Brown Beret leaders, are sentenced to 60 day jail terms for allegedly disturbing the peace (in connection with the school walkouts). They are then transferred, the week of the 28th, to the maximum security facilities at the Wayside Honor Ranch near Castaic. Another Brown Beret, Carlos Montez, was jailed earlier this week and charged with failure to respond to traffic citations.

In a statement following the arrest and jailing of its leaders, the Brown Berets said: "The police think they can destroy grassroots organizations like the Brown Berets by putting the leaders in jail, but they are wrong. The Man cannot destroy us by his harassment or his threats. Every time he tries to oppress us, we become more determined to resist and continue the struggle."

The Brown Berets opened a new office on May 5th at the corner of Brooklyn and Soto.

# THROUGH BROWN EYES

Residents of the 800 unit East Side Aliso Village, the first racially integrated low-cost housing project in the entire country, have set up a l5-man Task Force to bring an end to harassment of young Blacks by White officers (at the projects). The Task Force, including members of the Brown Berets, was organized on May 20.

Nearly 2,000 Chicanos turned out for a demonstration in Los Angeles on June 2, after 13 leaders of the Chicano Movement were indicted on charges of "conspiracy to commit a disturbance."

Among those arrested were Sal Castro, Lincoln High School teacher; Eliazar Risco, Editor of La Raza; David Sanchez, Prime Minister of the Brown Berets; Moctezuma Esperza, of U.M.A.S.; Joe Razo, of La Raza Newspaper; Cruz Olmeda, Chairman of the Brown Berets; Carlos Munoz, State Chairman of U.M.A.S.; Fred Lopez; Ralph Ramirez, of the Brown Berets; Richard Vigil; Pat Sanchez; Henry Gomez; and Carlos Montez, also of the Brown Berets.

# THROUGH BROWN EYES

The Requiem March (over the assassination of Senator Robert F. Kennedy) left from Obregon Park at about 6:00 pm on June 8, with about 1,000 in line. It more than doubled in size by the time it reached the East Los Angeles College Stadium.

Monitors of the march included Brown Berets.

Among the first "International acts" by the nationalistic Brown Berets (who still oppose all forms of oppression) was their involvement in the "Anti-Vietnam War" effort. On October 31, the Berets had Ron Rodriguez, a member-spokesman, speak for the group at a "U.S. OUT OF SOUTH EAST ASIA NOW" rally.

In September of this year, Sal Castro is barred from teaching in the Los Angeles School District because of walkout felony charges.

The Educational Issues Committee and other organizations sit-in at the Board of Education offices for 8 days, in October, in support of the reinstatement of Sal Castro.

At the end of the sit-in, 35 Chicanos are arrested for misdemeanors. Sal Castro is reinstated to teach.

Arsonists set fire to the headquarters of the Brown Berets about 3:00 am Christmas morning, burning furniture, charring walls, and breaking windows in the attack.

On May 20, the Brown Berets open the East Los Angeles Free Clinic, which offers free social, psychological and medical services.

Meanwhile, the Los Angeles County Grand Jury issues indictments against 10 Chicanos, including Brown Berets Ralph Ramirez and Carlos Montez on May 31, charging them with conspiracy to commit arson at the Biltmore Hotel where, on April 2!}, 1968, Governor Reagan spoke at the Nuevo Vistas.

1969

# THROUGH BROWN EYES

At the 16th of September "Independence" parade in Los Angeles, Brown Berets ride a 90MM Scorpion tank down Brooklyn Ave.

Chanting "Chicano Power" and led by sharp marching Brown Berets, nearly a thousand Chicanos marched into Obregon Park in East Los on December 20 in a Chicano Moratorium protest against the war in Vietnam. Another 500, predominantly young Chicanos, joined the marchers for a rally in the park.

The march was organized by a Chicano coalition composed mainly of the Brown Berets, Movimiento Estudiantil Chicano de Aztlan (MECHA), and the San José supporters of the Delano grape strike.

Carlos Montez, a Brown Beret spokesman at the rally, said "We're here to protest the high rate of Chicanos and to protest U. S. aggression against the people of Vietnam."

Through the march and rally, demonstrators greeted each other with shouts of "Viva La Raza". Speakers would yell out "Chicano" and the people answered "Power." It was a day for LA RAZA.

1970

The Berets also participated in a march down Atlantic Blvd. in Los Angeles, February 28. Also in attendance was Rodolfo "Corky" Gonzales, of the Crusade for Justice in Denver, Colorado.

All through the Brown Beret movement, "futurists" kept exerting their influence to move the Organization in a more positive and useful direction, with more accessibility to the Chicano community. Octaviano Quintero, a member of the San Diego Brown Berets, told more than 400 students, at an all-day conference on Chicano education, during the summer, that they must forego violence. "The Brown Berets need not be synonymous with violence, but should work within the community to teach younger children to help one another", he said.

1971

On April 17, ten women began picketing in front of the Pharr, Texas, Police Department, demanding the resignation of Officer Alfredo Ramirez, Sgt. Mateo Sandoval and Gilbert Zuniga. Approximately 30 onlookers gathered across the street from the police department, including 8 members of the Brown Berets. The Berets were in Pharr for the purpose of assisting the picketers in case of trouble.

The Brown Berets sponsored a Moratorium March and Rally, in November, to protest the repressive tactics of the Sheriff's Department against La Raza.

1972

Some 300 Chicanos marched Saturday, June 17, in Wilmington, to launch a summer of organizing in small minority communities. The march, sponsored by a coalition of groups and led by the Chicano Moratorium and the Brown Berets, passed through a Southern California housing project. The marchers ended up at Harbor Park to listen to various speakers.

On June 20, David Sanchez and approximately 4 uniformed Brown berets dedicated a monument at the Euclid Community Center, 3045 Whittier Boulevard, Los Angeles, California, to commemorate the Chicanos who died during the August 29, 1970, and January 31, 1971, Chicano Moratoriums in Los Angeles. He stated that the monument should become a landmark of when Chicanos stopped fighting Chicanos and became united to struggle together for their Civil Rights and better education. He asked everyone present to sacrifice himself for the betterment of the community. He mentioned that the monument marked what formerly had been El Camino Real and then became Whittier Boulevard, and that it had been erected through the efforts of the Brown Berets as another step in La Marcha de La Reconquista. Sanchez then asked everyone present to join him in a prayer in which he asked God to help them to obtain a better life, better education for the children, and to help them dedicate themselves to the community.

According to a press release issued June 26 at Las Cruces, New Mexico, by David Sanchez, the Brown Berets (who were continuing their marching into many small communities) were marching in protest of the injustices the undocumented worker faces before the U.S. Department of Immigration and Naturalization Service (I.N.S.). The Berets demanded that "racist practices of the I.N.S. cease immediately." They also protested maintenance of I.N.S. camps, illegal searches of Mexicans, and called for the disarming of the I.N.S. officers.

Fifty members of the National Brown Berets were part of the march from Tortugas, Nuevo Mexico, to El Paso, Tejas. The 45 mile march started on June 26, and went to the 28th of the same month.

About 30 members of the Brown Berets National Organization held a rally on July 01, in Cleveland Square in El Paso, to protest the unjust treatment of undocumented workers.

During the July rally, Brown Beret Prime Minister, David Sanchez said the following: The Brown Berets are a national organization with about 90 chapters throughout the country. The Brown Berets were founded in 1967. Not all youth who wear berets are members. The beret must have the insignia which reads "La Causa." Sanchez added that the Berets "are not militant, but a military-structured organization with discipline. We avoid being just a mob. We also discourage drinking and drugs." He concluded that the Berets "are peaceful, non-violent and productive."

# *THROUGH BROWN EYES*

On July 6th, David Sanchez and Jeronimo Ramirez Blanco conferred with Immigration and Naturalization Service and Border Patrol officials at the U.S. Court House building in El Paso, Tejas, between 10:00 and 11:00 am, at which time the Berets presented 11 concerns of discrimination against Mexicanos and Chicanos.

There were many other meetings, rallies, marches and demonstrations. I have included just these few because, first of all, I had direct sources to these incidents, and, secondly, because they serve my purpose. Con Safos.

# *THROUGH BROWN EYES*

---

## I **AM** DIFFERENT

Our Skins Are Different Colors

Our Foods Are Not The Same

You Even Hate To Talk To Me

Cause You Can't Pronounce My Name


Our Dances Are Also Different

Of Course That's Plain To See

But When I Dance It My Way

Why Should You Make Fun Of Me


You Show Discrimination

Prejudice And Bigotry

And Then You Turn Around And Say

That You Know What's Best For Me


I Live A Life So Different

From The One You Claim To See

My Life Is Filled With Happiness

And A Love That's Always Free

---

# *THROUGH BROWN EYES*

My Pride Is Very Great
And Very Hard To Please, You See
I Would Rather Die On My Feet
Than To Ever Live On My Knees!

- Juan M. Pérez

# THROUGH BROWN EYES

---

*Chapter Three*

## *LOS OTROS CAPITULOS DE LOS BROWN BERETS*

Another section of the Organization which found itself in the limelight, as it were, was the Brown Berets of New Mexico. I have included some of the materials I was fortunate to obtain from different sources (including the files of the F.B.I.) and from my own memory of what occurred in Nuevo Mexico during those early days.

On August lit, 1968, the Albuquerque Journal reported "A policeman shot and killed a man he thought was an auto thief behind a South Valley residence on the night of August 13.

"Police Captain Robert Bales, Albuquerque Police Department, said Officer Larry Ward shot Tommy Valles in the chest after Valles attacked him from a shed.

"A car which the police were chasing was not actually stolen, but belonged to the dead man's mother. The police said the car fitted the description of one reported missing.

"Captain Bales said Valles was chased by Officer Ward with for nearly half a mile before he ran into a shed.

"Valles ran into a dead-end area and attacked Officer Ward with a metal wedge. Officer Ward fired one shot hitting Valles in the chest. Officer Ward suffered a laceration on his chest where the wedge struck him."

---

# THROUGH BROWN EYES

On August 16, the New Mexico Brown Berets passed out literature on the same subject that had this to say:

"Tommy and Johnny Valles were driving west on Bridge Street in their mother's car about 7:00 pm on August 13th. Ike Saavedra was with them. Just before reaching the approach to Barelas bridge, they noticed a police car following them and for some reason they decided to get away. They went west on Bridge for about two miles, turned left on Goff for about a block, and got stuck in the sand (the papers describe this as a wild zig zag car chase through the South Valley). The three got out of the car. Saavedra stayed by the car. Johnny Valles ran to the Arenal ditch and then gave himself up to police officers. Tommy Valles ran on farther and hid in a shed. Police officer Larry Ward chased Tommy Valles on foot and saw him go into the shed.

"Up to this point the only charges that could be brought against the three were speeding or reckless driving, although police later claimed that they thought the car was stolen. The police officers made no attempt to talk to Tommy Valles in the shed or to try to get him out. They did not ask Tommy's brother or Ike Saavedra to persuade him to come out. They knew he was unarmed. Officer Ward went into the shed and shot Tommy Valles in the chest at point blank range. He died immediately.

"Some time later, policeman Ward claimed that Valles had thrown something at him and even checked in at a local hospital with a minor cut to establish this claim. The police failed to notify the Valles family that they had killed Tommy -they first heard it on the radio.

"We are here to do something about the senseless murder of Tommy Valles by an Albuquerque police officer. Valles was shot while being investigated for suspicion of car theft. He was driving his mother's car.

# THROUGH BROWN EYES

"He was unarmed and no threat to the policeman. He was cornered in a shed where he could easily have been made to come out. He was given no warning that he would be shot if he did not give up. Yet he was shot and killed by a policeman acting as cop, judge, jury, and executioner. Is this what is meant by law and order'?

"Chief Shaver said "our investigation shows it appears justified," and "those things happen." The District Attorney asked the State Police to investigate the City Police in an obvious whitewash. The press made the three men sound like criminals that deserved shooting anyway. The cover-up has started.

"But this is not the first time it has happened - and it won't be the last time, unless something is done right now. Policemen must learn that they have no right to shoot people for suspicion of a minor offense. No one will be safe if all a cop has to do is make up a story and say he was justified.

"WHAT WE WANT

We hope the family of Tommy Valles will bring charges against Officer Ward but this is beyond our control. Therefore, we make the following demands:

1. Immediate dismissal of Officer Ward.

2. Creation of a legitimate civilian review board that fairly represents the Mexican-American community of Albuquerque.

"WHY WE HAVE COME TO OLD TOWN------

We the New Mexico Brown Berets, organized ourselves to be of service to the Mexican-American community. We feel we can do this by eliminating injustice wherever it occurs, but especially in our own communities. We have chosen Old Town to make our stand because, for many visitors and newcomers to Albuquerque, it

# THROUGH BROWN EYES

represents the Mexican-American community and cultural cooperation. We hope that many people will see us and find out that there is still terrible injustice in Albuquerque and New Mexico.

"We hope our demands will be met immediately, but we are ready to carry our message to the people who visit Old Town indefinitely, and even find better ways if this does not work. We welcome the support of any person or group who believes in justice and harmony for New Mexico.

BROWN BERETS of New Mexico , 1315 Bridge St. SW"

On August 20, the Albuquerque Tribune reported that "Gilberto Ballejos, the Spokesman of the Brown Berets of New Mexico (BBNM) was interviewed on August 20, 1968. He described the BBNM as a Spanish-American group which is a "civic organization." He said it started to organize here a few months ago after the poor people's March on Washington, D.C. It is still organizing, he said. Ballejos stated Spanish-Americans from Albuquerque met a group of Brown Berets from California while in Washington. Some of the Albuquerqueans became interested and came back early to start an organization of their own.

"Ballejos refused to disclose the number in the group or the names of the members. He said "Our representatives are the only ones that know the membership of our organization for reasons of personal protection from the police.

We meet at no specific time or place that is predetermined, but in secret; for instance, at one time we met under the Rio Grande Bridge. Only persons of Spanish-American decent can be members of the Brown Berets." He also declared members do not call themselves Spanish-American or Mexican-American but only Mexicans, because they do not feel like they are being treated like Americans.

The paper went on to say that Gilberto Ballejos edits "El Papel," a militant paper published in English, which he says is the property of the BBNM. He said the purpose of "El Papel" is to tell the Spanish-American side of the story. An issue of "El Papel" devoted much space to national affairs, attacking President Johnson, Vice-President Hubert Humphrey, and Senator Eugene McCarthy. A picture of Humphrey showed him with an Adolf Hitler mustache. It referred to Senator McCarthy as "Hygiene." A picture of Revolutionary Ernesto "Che" Guevara is carried on the front."

On August 20, the Albuquerque Journal reported that Gilberto Ballejos said the Brown Berets are organized in 15 sections or neighborhoods. He refused to disclose the number or the names of any members. He did advise that three members from each section meet to vote on what action or program the BBNM will undertake, so there must be at least 45 members, if Ballejos is correct. During the demonstrations in Old Town Plaza, about 50 persons were observed marching and carrying signs. Most of them were young, in their teens and 20's.

It went on to report that on August 20, "A hard-eyed contingent of militants, including the BBNM and land grant leader Reis Lopez

Tijerina, made three demands for police reform to City Commissioners at a meeting held Monday, August 19, 1968."

"On August 22, the Albuquerque Journal reported that "Gilberto Ballejos, the spokesman for the BBNM, in an interview by a member of the Staff of the "Albuquerque Journal" advised "We formed the Brown Berets for the same reason the Lions Club organized. We formed to protect ourselves, our interests, our lives if necessary. We are trying to do something about things like the

injustices in the schools. Our members don't have jobs; they are mostly dropout, under-educated and unemployed; the police are on our backs."

"The BBNM," said Ballejos, "are not asking for anything unreasonable. We are asking for a police review board comprised of three Spanish-Americans, two Indians and one black, plus five members appointed by the Commission. We're asking for the suspension of Officer Ward until the board can review this case, and we're asking for a psychiatric examination for all policemen."

The BBNM is a civic organization formed to help Mexican-Americans. He said there was no connection between the people in the neighborhoods and those in power. He blamed the newspapers for this lack, claiming "When you want to know what people think you use your own information, you ask Mexicans who are afraid of losing their jobs, so they tell you what you want to know."

# THROUGH BROWN EYES

"Ballejos said the BBNM has no connection with the Alianza Federal de Mercedes (AFDM). However, Reies Lopez Tijerina, who was subsequently interviewed, said the two groups have the same objectives. Tijerina described the BBNM as a group exclusively for the younger Alianza members, "something to keep them busy."

On August 27, the Albuquerque Journal reported that "At a meeting of the City Commissioners held on August 26, 1968, leaders of militant BBNM rejected the Commission's proposals for improved relations between Albuquerque police and the community. They made only a brief appearance at a meeting, and walked out after advising the Commissioners that their actions were completely unacceptable. On September 04, the Albuquerque Journal reported that "Residents of the Los Giegos and Duranes areas met with the City Commission during the 6th series of "Gripe-ins" held at Our Lady of Guadalupe Church in Albuquerque on September 3, 1968. The peaceful meeting was marred only by a walkout of about 25 persons led by the BBNM, whose leaders again expressed their dissatisfaction with the failure of the City Commission to support a civilian review board of Police Department activities.

The October 4, 1968, issue of the New Mexico Lobo, a daily campus publication of the University of New Mexico, contained an article concerning an agreement of the Radical Rush, a loose coalition of University groups, to work with the Brown berets in gaining signatures on a petition asking for a recall election of the Albuquerque City Commission. The article noted that the Brown Berets' gripes against the city police centered upon complaints of police brutality in the poor neighborhoods. The article noted that Gilberto Ballejos, Beret leader, claimed there had been five killings by policemen in the Albuquerque area in the last two years, and that all those killed were Chicano. The article reported there were about thirty members in the Brown Berets, which had been organized approximately for four months.

Although it was felt that the petition for a recall election would fail, it was stressed that the major purpose in getting the signatures on the petition would be to inform the people of Albuquerque about what is really going on in the city.

The October III, 1968, issue of the Albuquerque Journal contained an article concerning a weekend conference at the D. H. Lawrence Ranch near Taos, New Mexico, of community leaders, students, and University of New Mexico faculty and administrative officials. The article reported that, an unscheduled appearance on Saturday night of a group of Brown Berets led by Gilberto Ballejos brought about some serious discussions in the closing hours of the conference. The Brown Berets came to the University owned ranch from a conference of their own at nearby San Cristobal Ranch, and Ballejos was allowed fifteen minutes to make his presentation. Ballejos complained about New Mexico's population of "Spanish-Americans" in attendance at the University.

The November 14, 1968, issue of The New Mexican a daily newspaper published in Santa Fe, New Mexico, contained an article announcing that a demonstration to protest "the rotten politicians and the rich people who have denied Spanish-Americans of their civil rights" was scheduled for noon, Saturday 16. The paper reported that Los Comancheros and the Brown Berets of Albuquerque were sponsoring the demonstration. A spokesman for the two groups announced that another demonstration was scheduled for Sunday the 17th at the District Court in Albuquerque, where Reies Lopez Tijerina, leader of the Alianza Federal de Mercedes, and ten other defendants were on trial.

# THROUGH BROWN EYES

The November 18, 1968, issue of the Albuquerque Journal contained a news item which reported that sixty demonstrators, proclaiming support of land grant leader Reies Lopez Tijerina and his followers, who were on trial, paraded before the Bernalillo County Courthouse on Sunday, November 17th. The article quoted Brown Berets leader Gilberto Ballejos as saying the demonstration meant to raise two major issues: (1) the question of venue; that is why the trial was not being held in Tierra Amarilla, New Mexico, as it should be (for the reader's information, on October 26, 1966, Reies Lopez Tijerina and four other members of the Alianza Federal de Mercedes were charged in Federal Court with assaulting a Federal Officer and conversion of Government property, as a result of their land grant claims; also On June 05, 1967, Reies Lopez Tijerina and 19 others were charged in State Court with kidnapping and assault with intent to commit felonies, resulting from entering the Tierra Amarilla, New Mexico, Courthouse with firearms and forcibly holding hostages and shooting law enforcement officers. Charges against all but eleven were subsequently dismissed, and the eleven were awaiting trial; finally, the Alianza Federal de Mercedes was incorporated in New Mexico on October 08, 1963, with the purpose of acquainting heirs of all Spanish Land Grants with their rights under the Treaty of Guadalupe-Hidalgo. Reies Lopez Tijerina was the groups President and the name of the organization was changed on August 19, 1967, to Alianza Federal de Pueblos (Libres - JMP); and (2) that one third of the jury should include Mexican-Americans who are really representative of Mexican-Americans, not Tio Tomas' (Uncle Toms). The article reported that the demonstration included Brown Berets, Red Berets, Comancheros, and placard bearers of individual commitment as well as others.

The December 06, 1968, issue of the Albuquerque Journal contained an article which stated that a Brown Berets deputy claimed the leader of the Brown Berets had been expelled. Berets member Alfonso Sanchez, who described himself as second in command to Gilberto Ballejos, claimed that the Brown Berets voted Ballejos out of their Organization during a special meeting on Wednesday, December Oil, 1968. Sanchez said he and other Beret members became disenchanted with Ballejos because he "preached hate and made racist talk." The article continued that Ballejos appeared undismayed by the news of his alleged expulsion; he claimed to know nothing about it, and stated that it sounded as if the others wanted publicity. He said that if they wanted their own organization, it was all right with him, but complained that he had not heard about it before they called the newspapers.

The following article appeared in the March 06, 1969, issue of the "Albuquerque News," a weekly newspaper published every Thursday in Albuquerque, New Mexico: "If there has been confusion, mystery, and uncertainty over Reies Lopez Tijerina and his Alianza Federal de Mercedes, these in no way compare to the myths and rumors that spring up when a militant group of young Mexicans from the barrios of the Southwest who call themselves the Brown Berets are mentioned.

"Yet of all the Nationalist and radical currents in the Mexican community, the Berets are perhaps the most important and the most conscious of what they are after.

"They have a program, an objective and what seems to me to be a clear understanding of what it takes to organize the Mexican people in an effort to turn back the tide of a history of 120 years of what they call "degradation" and what they see as a "slow but purposeful genocide.

"The Berets are a rapidly growing national movement.

"While there is no single national leadership, national committee or center, the Brown Berets, allied with groups such as the Black Berets and Northern New Mexico's Los Comancheros, are emerging all over the West.

"In New Mexico, the Berets seem to have sunk deep roots into the barrios of Albuquerque and to have formed other groups in Santa Fe, Las Vegas, Espanola, Belen, and Socorro. They project organizational drives in southern and southwestern New Mexico.

"What kind of groups are these Berets? What is their social base and the quality of their leadership? Are they a reform group, or are they a serious revolutionary movement ready to pass from acceptable to unacceptable tactics, from peaceful to non-peaceful methods? What is their perspective for the Southwest and how do they see its relationship to the rest of Latin America? What do these people think of the potential of decent Anglos who want justice?

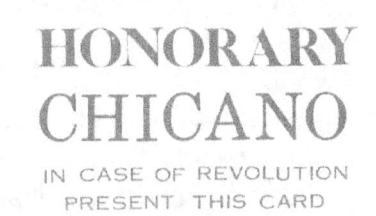

HONORARY CHICANO

IN CASE OF REVOLUTION PRESENT THIS CARD TO A BROWN BERET

"These are some of the questions that I discussed with a group of Beret organizers recently. There were eight in all - two women and six men. They ranged from their late teens to their mid-thirties, from high school drop-outs to a college graduate. Most of them were native to Albuquerque, but one was born in Rio Arriba County. There were veterans of front-line fighting in Vietnam and former convicts among them. They were all, to a man and woman, products of the barrios - working class in origin and composition.

"There was no leader among them.

"They function as a genuinely working collective of equals.

"After listening to them for several hours, I was left with three general impressions. First, these people are deadly serious and fully committed revolutionaries. Second, they come closer to forming a revolutionary vanguard organization than any other group I have seen or talked with or studied in this country. Third, they are a group of potential revolutionaries who have a clear understanding of what their problems are, what is required to meet those problems, how to organize a movement and mobilize people around those problems while they build a revolutionary consciousness and commitment.

"I think the day of the headline hunting patron, speaking in the name of the Mexican people, whether he is a self-styled radical or a member of an official government agency, is drawing to an end. Albuquerque lawyer Lorenzo Tapia may not have known how prophetic he was when he recently told the U. S. Civil Rights Commission that he didn't know how long Mexican "leaders" could keep their people "under wraps." He warned that Mexicans are beccoming increasingly militant. It is the function of the Berets, as I understand it, to cut away the base of this older leadership and increase the militancy, forging it into a major movement. This is their aim at the present.

"How do the Berets operate?

"They have a six man coordination board, each man equals the other. One of their number is chosen as a public spokesman, but he remains fully the creature of the board, subject to their decisions. At the moment that spokesman is Gilbert Ballejos. But there are no leaders or deputies as such. Each board member functions as an organizer in his own barrio and is chosen from his barrio. He has around him a cadre of workers who in turn have real roots in their barrios and are able to activate or mobilize those they are working with when necessary.

# THROUGH BROWN EYES

At their first demonstration in August, the group mobilized over three hundred people. Today, after six months of quiet, hard organizing, they feel their strength and influence to be far greater.

"Each barrio organizer knows his own cadre but not all those who are involved in the movement. Organizers from one barrio do not know the depths of members or personnel in other barrios.

"General activities are coordinated by the board, but it is felt that this bottom-up structure lessens somewhat the dangers of police infiltration and disruptive activities by those who may be opposed to the Organization and what it stands for.

"Communications are also maintained throughout the country between various Beret and allied organizations. In fact, several local Berets spent some time towards the end of last year in California, where they talked with their brothers of the coast.

"The Beret program speaks of the "unity of all our people regardless of age, income or political philosophy." The issues around which such unity is to be forged are those of reasserting the dignity of La Raza, the reclamation of the land, the restoration of the full equality of their language and the teaching of the history of this region like it really was and is. (One of those I spoke to, a Mexican high school girl, says she was forbidden to take Spanish by a school official in this state which legally guarantees bilingual education.)

"If the Berets intend to reassert their rights as a people, they have to engage in the politics of power. And they have made very clear to me that this means repudiation of the old political parties, the Democratic and Republican parties, as well as the moribund parties of the left, like the Communists, or even "independent" parties tied to a purely electoral outlook. The politics of power requires deep organizing - house by house and barrio by barrio. Only out of such work can a mass base be built. The group says it hopes to reason with the Anglos in power, but "if reason fails we will be ready to fight if necessary."

"They do not include in their vision of la Raza Unida those whom they believe to be vendideros (sell-outs) (actually the word is spelled vendidos - JMP); they mention such men as Joseph M. Montoya and presidential appointee Vicente T Ximenes in this category.

"The political outlook is not limited to the Southwest alone. One of those present suggested as an accurate description of their internationalist outlook the slogan, "From Tierra Amarilla to Tierra Del Fuego" "They desire a peaceful change, but they will not let what they see as liberal clichés of "peaceful change" and "non-violence" become an excuse for delaying further the return of their rights. "We have been patient too long. Patience is no longer for us," they say.

"We will not fight any Raza group, and we will lend our support to all Raza groups that can get our people together for the long struggle ahead" seemed to be a recurrent theme. Their sympathies with militants like the Crusade for Justice operating in Colorado and northern New Mexico were obvious. They also refuse to attack the Alianza, pointing out its successes and contribution.

"Why do the Berets exist? Are they the nihilists some Anglo liberal academics would have us believe all radicals are?

The word "why" is not so difficult to answer. Too many of us claim to be concerned about people, about man, but not enough are concerned about the Mexican, the Lag} from the barrio or the campesino from the north. Too many people don't give a damn about grazing permits which are denied to shepherds whose families lived in northern New Mexico for 300 years. Too few of us care that starvation is a reality in Rio Arriba County.

"There are other reasons, too, other injustices, but things like this are why there was a Tierra Amarilla disturbance. They are why Los Comancheros, the Crusade for Justice and the Brown Berets have come into being. They are why young militants from the north and barrios are tired of patience and will appeal to reason only a little longer while they prepare the groundwork for what must follow if their appeals fall on deaf ears.

"Who has listened to them?

"Not the Church, was the consensus among most of the organizers -

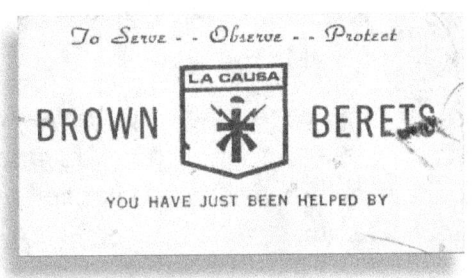

"Not the Church which has never even given us a bishop from among our own people." Not the liberal lawyers, who exact what seem to them huge fees for defending Mexican militants. Not the white businessman, who won't hire Mexicans. (A veteran of the war in Vietnam claimed that of the Mexicans who fought alongside of him there only two have been able to find jobs since they came home - both in menial work.)

"To serve, observe, and protect" is their motto.

"To serve "To give vocal as well as physical support to those people and causes which will help the people of the Mexican-American communities."

"To observe 'to keep a watchful eye on Federal, state, city and private agencies which deal with the Mexican-Americans, especially the law-enforcement agencies.

"To protect 'To guarantee and secure the rights of the Mexican-American by all means necessary. How far we must go in order to protect those rights is dependent upon those in power. If those Anglos in power are willing to do this in a peaceful and orderly process, then we will be only too happy to accept this way. Otherwise, we will be forced to other alternatives.'

"They have chosen the symbol of the Brown Beret 'because it is a symbol of the love and pride we have for our race and for the color of our skin. The Brown Beret also acts as a symbol of unity among chichanos.' (I believe the reporter was trying to spell Chicanos – JMP).

In any case, the reporter, JAMES A. KENNEDY, probably came closer than any non-Chicano in actually reporting the real feelings of the existence, cause, motivation, and incentive of the Brown Berets.

As you have seen so far, being a member, chapter, associate, or in any way affiliated with the Brown Berets is a hard road to travel, but one whose rewards in the end are dependent on how it was traveled.

Another prominently active Chapter during this time period was the Omard Chapter. I included only a few examples for your information.

In August, 1968, the Omard California Chapter of the Brown Berets appeared at a meeting of the Omard City Council and presented a petition protesting police tactics and calling for establishment of a police review board and an investigation of the police department by the California State Attorney General.

Officers of the Berets identified themselves as: Andres Herrera, 22, Prime Minister; Robert Gonzales, 20, Minister of Public Records; and Armando Jesus Lopez, 22, Minister of Public Relations.

# THROUGH BROWN EYES

On January 24, 1969, 25 individuals, four of whom were Brown Berets, picketed in front of the Ventura County Court House. The picketing began at 9:15 am and ended at 1:00 pm. They protested the prosecution of Robert Gene Estrada, a juvenile, on burglary charges.

This group then demonstrated at the Omard Police Department and other civic buildings, protesting the shooting of Lorenzo Torres on January 22, 1969, by Omard police officers during an alleged burglary.

The January 29, 1969, edition of the newspaper "Star Free Press," Ventura, California, contained an article entitled "Brown Berets Demand Firing of Omard Chief." It states that a group led by Brown Beret, Andres Herrera, on January 28, "flooded into the Omard City Council chambers and demanded the firing of Chief of Police Al Jewell, suspension of three officers, and the establishment of a police review board.

These demands were not met; but, the City Council agreed to investigate the shooting of a burglary suspect, Lorenzo Torres, which triggered these complaints.

On February 05, 1969, Armando Lopez, Minister of Education, Omard Chapter of the Brown Berets, spoke at the Rio Mesa High School, in Omard, and stated that the Brown Berets are meant to be a well-disciplined group and outlined the following activities:

1.) The establishment of a Mexican-American studies course in Moorpark College.

2.) We are consultants for the Omard Elementary School District.

3.) We are concerned with the law enforcement of the City of Omard.

4.) We want to form a Police Review Board to work on problems of malpractice and communication with Omard Police.

5.) We form a liaison with community service agencies and people in our community.

6.) We are militant but we are not violent - we want to bring social change in a non-violent manner.

Kansas City, Missouri, is one of the last places I would have looked for in my search for additional information on the Brown Berets, but I was surprised to find out that they did indeed exist in that city and were constructive. I also included some of the activities of theirs in this chapter of the book.

On May 29, 1969, the following article appeared in the Kansas City Star, a daily Kansas City, Missouri, newspaper, under the heading "Police Bias Against Mexicans."

"The chairman of the Brown Berets, an organization of youths of Mexican extraction, last night charged that police have been harassing members of his community.

"Charles J. Carillo made the statement in connection with the recent arrest of two 17 year old youths. They are being held in jail in connection with the attempted arson of public buildings the night of May 19, when fire bombs were thrown at a police garage, fire station and barber shop.

"The two youths are Benjamin Escareno, 1123 West Twenty-Fourth Street, and Anthony David Rios, 3820 Montgall Avenue. Preliminary hearings have been set for Tuesday.

"When asked about the May l9 incidents Carillo said 'We feel that this is another case in point of police harassment on individuals from the oppressed minority groups in Kansas City. We feel that there must be a strong platform developed to preserve the constitutional, social and civil rights of the Mexican-Americans.

"The purpose of his organization, Carillo said, 'is to promote the furtherance of social justice and civil rights for the Mexican-American youth and to get residents of the West side to participate in a constructive program that will benefit everyone in the community.'

"We believe that we should be allowed the opportunity to apply the principles of self-determination; that is, the right to make our own decisions and to participate in the decisions which affect our daily lives.

"He denied, as reported earlier, that the purpose of the organization was to solicit money, especially government funds, for their organization."

# THROUGH BROWN EYES

On August 12, 1969, the following article appeared in the Kansas City Times, in Missouri, under the heading "Youths Call Fund Dispersal 'Unfair.'"

"Two Mexican-American youth groups on the West side have asked that all youth program funds allocated to the area be stopped until they can be evenly divided between the Mexican-American and Negro populations.

"In a letter to officials of the Human Resources Corporation, the Regional Office of Economic Opportunity and the City, representatives of the Brown Berets and the Guadalupe Youth group charged discrimination in the division of funds.

"The Mexican-American youths said that the problem arose first when Miss Rosa A. Suarez, area I Poverty Center Director, recognized the Pennway Youth group as the planning group for the youth program in the area.

"'Whenever it seemed that Chicano (Mexican-American) youth were getting organized, making progress and gaining the power, the Poverty Center Director, Miss Rosa A. Suarez, would interfere and take her usual position by siding with Pennway,' the letter said.

"The Chicago (I believe that the reporter meant Chicano - JMP) youths said that the youth advisory board then hired nine of its own members to work in the Pennway summer program and gave only two jobs to the Guadalupe youths.

"Both have centers, known as youth lounges, with television sets and pool tables. But the Pennway Center had money to conduct tours and trips for its youth while Guadalupe did not, they added. Only occasionally did Pennway provide space for Guadalupe youths on the trips, they said.

# THROUGH BROWN EYES

"The Chicano youths said that they had talked last Tuesday to Vernon Thompson, director of the H. R. C. Youth Program, and had been assured that the program would be stopped until it could be corrected.

"Chester Stovall, H. R. C. Executive Director, said he would see that the problems were straightened out, they added.

"Others who signed the letter were Benjamin Escareno and Charlie J. Carillo for the Brown Berets, and Eddie Munoz, Anthony J. Aguirre and Robert Vaca for the Guadalupe Youth group."

An article appearing in the Kansas City Star newspaper on September l6, 1969, revealed that approximately 150 students of West Junior High School, Kansas City, Missouri, staged a peaceful demonstration on same date as above in observance of Mexican Independence Day. The demonstration was led by the Brown Berets. The principal speaker was a Charles Lona, Chairman of the Raza Education Committee of the Brown Berets. He explained that the demonstration was to point out the plight of Mexican-American youth in the educational system and expose students to the Mexican Brown Power movement which is spreading throughout the Southwest.

The demonstration was completely peaceful. The students mainly presented dances, songs, and other acts based on Mexican-American culture.

Charles Lona mentioned other activities of the Brown Berets, such as the Berets being the "palace guards" of all Mexican-American organizations throughout the United States attempting to bring equal rights to the Mexican-Americans. He stated that the Brown Berets in Kansas City were marshals for a parade held on November 22, 1969, in Kansas City, by numerous Mexican-American groups, and they prevented disorders during this parade and a later demonstration including the National Chicanos, United Mexicans and Mexican-American youth organizations.

Also, Cesar Chavez, Director of the United Farm Workers Organizing Committee, from Sacramento, California, participated in this demonstration.

"The Brown Berets purpose," adds Lona, "is to protect, guarantee, and secure rights of all Mexican Americans, in schooling, housing, and employment." He went on to say that the Brown Berets in Kansas City are not affiliated with any national organization; however, they may attempt to obtain a charter if such a national organization is set up.

Lona wants the Brown Berets to expose Chicano youth to La Causa. He stated La Causa means "the cause" and Chicano is any Mexican-American working with the cause. He stated they also want to emphasize to the young Mexican-Americans that they are neither Black nor White, but Brown, and have different problems than other minority groups.

Let's move now to the far West of the United States to Oregon, there the Berets have existed as mostly a support group, but existed nevertheless.

The Brown Berets of Oregon consisted of approximately 23 members at one point. They were organized by, and were led by Emilio Ray Verdugo. Activities of the organization had been limited to small demonstrations and some picketing in support of a lettuce boycott sponsored by the United Farm Workers of California.

# THROUGH BROWN EYES

Member of the Brown berets have participated in demonstrations sponsored by other organizations.

An article appeared in the October 03, 1970, issue of The Oregonian, a Portland, Oregon, daily newspaper, which described a confrontation between law enforcement officers and members of the Oregon Brown Berets during an attempt by the Berets to "occupy" the abandoned Camp Adair Air Force Base, Corvallis, Oregon.

Members of the Berets taking place in this confrontation were Emilio Ray Verdugo, Ruben Rios Hernandez, George Louis Montemayor, Samuel Sanchez, Peter Hernandez and Israel Vasquez. No violence occurred during this confrontation.

There were a number of individuals who were known to be members of the Brown Berets attending the University of Oregon at Eugene, Oregon. The Brown Berets had not sponsored any rallies or demonstrations at the University, but had participated in demonstrations and rallies sponsored by other groups. The Brown Berets operated primarily as the Chicano Student Union (CSU) although all members of the CSU are not Berets. The Brown Berets Chapter at the University of Oregon was formed shortly after a Symposium on Racism held at the University during October, 1970.

KALAMAZOO: (quoting from a document from the FBI, dated 08-30-71, file 4157-7557) "Brown Berets, a small group of Chicanos (young Mexican-Americans) became active in Kalamazoo, Michigan, in January, 1971. Berets formed a coalition with White activists and advocated fire bombing and other direct action to achieve goals. Three Brown Beret members arrested during riotous disturbance 2/17/71.

During Spring, 1971 Berets continued criticism of local government and treatment of Mexican-American citizens in Kalamazoo. Beret leader facing charges of carrying a concealed weapon and assaulting a police officer hired by city government to work in community relations."

Officers of the Kalamazoo Brown Berets were identified as Richard "Ki Ki" Sanchez, Thomas Sanchez, and Isabell Torres Olivarez on the Central Committee. The Ministers were Armando Martinez, Minister of Information; Isabell Torres Olivarez, Minister of Treasury; Michael Gutierrez, Minister of Housing; Mario Cruz, Minister of Education; and Thomas Sanchez, Minister of Employment. Nine others were blacked out of the above mentioned document.

The March 30, 1971, edition of the Kalamazoo Gazette contained an article by Arthur Sills regarding the appearance of the Brown Berets at the Kalamazoo City Commission meeting on March 29, which in part stated: "Enrico (Ki Ki) Sanchez, a member of the Central Committee of the Brown Berets, said the Commissioners would sit there and listen to the Chicanos young and old, talk. 'You might sound good in public,' he told the commissioners, 'but when you get back behind closed doors, nothing is done about it. 'I'm not a racist in reverse,' said Sanchez, 'but I'm not going to look up to a white man who has been putting me down all his life.'

"'A lot of Chicanos are getting fed up with the way they are being treated in this All-American city,' said Sanchez. His brother, Thomas Sanchez, criticized treatment of young Mexican-Americans by the police and courts.

"'Police, putting you in jail, beat you up and judges say you can't get out of jail until you pay big bonds,' he said."

The June 08, 1971, issue of the Kalamazoo Gazette contained an article regarding the Brown Berets which states as follows:

"Kalamazoo's Chicano citizens want a place to call their own.

# THROUGH BROWN EYES

"And so far the City of Kalamazoo hasn't been able to deliver the goods.

"Representing the local corps of the Brown berets and the Latin American Steering Committee, Thomas Sanchez of 1622 N. Burdick, came before the City Commissioners Monday night for a progress report on how the search goes.

"It does not go well was the response.

"The Berets and the steering committee had met with city officials several weeks ago. One of the suggestions that came out of the gathering was the establishment of a headquarters where Spanish-speaking Kalamazooans could assemble as a combination social club and service agency.

"'We haven't given up the idea,' said City Manager James Caplinger, 'but we just haven't located any appropriate city-owned building yet.'

"A second recommendation called for the structuring of bi-lingual (English and Spanish) classes in the Kalamazoo school system. That matter belongs before the Kalamazoo Board of Education, the city manager said. But he also suggested that possibly such a program could be set up through the Kalamazoo Parks and Recreation Department's summer activities.

"The request drew some comment from Vice Mayor Gilbert Bradley, similar to remarks which he made last week when he opposed an ordinance to revamp the Community Relations Department.

"'We are on the threshold of something beautiful in Kalamazoo,' he said, 'but we keep letting these wonderful opportunities slip right through our hands.'

"Bradley explained that the Spanish speaking people 'want a place of their own so they can relate to people of their own kind.'

"Carlos Watson of 217 Monroe, a Kalamazoo College faculty member, suggested that the city tap the four institutions of higher learning in the community to aid in dealing with the problems of the migrants.

"A second Brown Beret, Abel Sanchez, read a proposal to commissioners which requested that the city provide a bus for field trips, provide some office space for Chicano project and programs, and adopt an ordinance declaring a 'Chicano Week.'

In July, 1971, the City Manager of Kalamazoo announced that Richard "Ki Ki" Sanchez had been hired by the city and placed in the City Personnel office.

Further, the city manager noted Sanchez will have the task of working with the City Community Relations Department in an effort to improve living and social conditions among Mexican-American residents of the city.

# THROUGH BROWN EYES

*Chapter Four*

## *LA CHICANA*

When deciding to write this chapter, I had a lot of problems with how to approach it. I tried to think of some exceptional thing that some female Beret member had done and couldn't think of any. Now don't get me wrong, I don't mean that no female member has ever done anything exceptional, but, also, I couldn't think of any exceptional thing that a male member had done either.

What I am leading to is: Brown Berets work as a collective.

What one member accomplishes in the Movement, is also accomplished by the Organization, which actually gets most of the credit.

Now there are many accomplishments by members, but this is done in their capacity as Brown Berets. So it is the Organization that is providing the member as a service of the group, and in return, backs the members in their functions within the movement.

Members, regardless of sex, are expected to be active to whatever capacity they can, but active nevertheless. When "on duty", whatever member is best capable of handling the required function is automatically expected to do so. So, when a member is doing something exceptional, she or he is just doing her/his duty.

Whatever "reward" the member gets usually comes from the Organization in form of respect and sometimes higher rank and/or positions.

Another point is that the Organization totally disregards issues that are solely male or female. Policy says that La Causa needs our total dedication. The liberation of Aztlan is to be the members' primary goal, so any issue or personal preference which interferes with that goal is to be disregarded.

The Brown Berets do have a male, macho image which no doubt causes many persons to wrongfully assume that the Organization is made up only of men.

Chicanas have been a part of the Brown Berets since the beginning - at San Catalina Island, on the "Caravana de la

# *THROUGH BROWN EYES*

Reconquista", at the marches, at the demonstrations, the rallies, the meetings, and to serve La Raza.

In Dallas, both male and female members have publicly represented the Brown Berets, and even so, the "macho" image is still there.

At the time of this writing, there are exactly the same number of Chicanas in the Organization as there are Chicanos, in Dallas.

Organizational Rules and Regulations apply equally to all members. I have included the "Revised, 1980, Rules and Regulations of the Dallas Brown Berets" for your information and inspection.

"The purpose of the Brown Berets is summed up in its motto:

TO SERVE To give vocal as well as physical support to those people and causes which will help the Chicano community.

TO OBSERVE To keep a watchful eye on all federal, state, city, and private agencies which deal with the Chicano community, especially the "law" enforcement agencies.

TO PROTECT To protect, guarantee, and secure the rights of the Chicano by any means necessary. How far we must go in order to protect these rights is dependent upon those in power. We are prepared to defend our positions by using the same response which is imposed on us.

WHY A BROWN BERET?

# THROUGH BROWN EYES

The brown beret was chosen because it is a symbol of the love and pride we have in our race and in the color of our skin. The brown beret also acts as a symbol among Chicanos.

THE OBJECTIVES OF THE DALLAS BROWN BERETS SHALL BE:

1) To identify specific problems in the Chicano community.

2) To expose those problems, so as to make the Chicano community aware of their severity.

3) To assist the victims of these problems.

4) To fulfill the By-laws of Los Brown Berets de Tejas, Aztlan Organization.

5) To struggle for the liberation of Aztlan.

6) None other.

THE ISSUES THAT THE ORGANIZATION SHALL BE INVOLVED IN ARE:

1) Police brutality and the misuse of authority by law enforcement officials.

2) Dual standards in the justice system.

3) Those issues in which the Organization will serve the Chicano community in a positive manner.

4) Those issues selected by Los Brown Berets de Tejas, Aztlan Organization.

5) The struggle for the liberation of Aztlan.

6) None other.

THE SERVICES THE ORGANIZATION WILL PROVIDE ARE:

1) To assist police brutality and misuse of authority victims in the preparation of their case(s) against the police department.

2) To assist in and/or provide to persons, or groups, the technical methods of operation concerning the legal and proper way to conduct demonstrations.

3) To provide referral assistance in cases not listed above.

4) To publish and distribute information on events relating to the

Movement.

5) Any other service decided by Los Brown Berets de Tejas, Aztlan Organization.

6) None other.

MEMBERSHIP

Active Membership

1) Must be Chicano.

2) Must be old enough to make her/his own decisions.

3) Must accept and apply self to the philosophy and regulations without exception.

Supportive Membership

1) Must be Chicano.

2) Must pay minimum of $5.00 per month as membership tee.

3) May attend and participate in regular meetings, but will have no vote on any matter.

4) Supportive membership will be kept private upon request.

Marshalls

1) May be any race.

2) May assist in any and all demonstrations and/or activities.

3) Must take a one-time course in the implementation and organizing of legal demonstrations and activities.

Regulations

1) A Brown Beret will always demonstrate self-discipline.

2) A Brown Beret will respect the beret itself, for it represents La Raza, Unity, Carnalismo, and the Organization.

3) A Brown Beret will never fight with another Brown Beret or Chicano, except in self-defense.

4) No Brown Beret will indulge in narcotics.

5) A Brown Beret will always preach and demonstrate Carnalismo.

6) Berets (the cap) will not be worn while the member is drinking alcoholic beverages or is under any such influence.

ORGANIZATIONAL PHILOSOPHY

We believe that La Raza has the right to control its own destiny. That we have the right to choose which government we are to serve, and not be imposed with an alien government which discriminates against us solely because of the color of our skin, and denies us equal protection under it's "law." And also, deprives us of the opportunity to economically sustain ourselves independently, because of racism. We believe in self-determination, and that belief is Aztlan.

I must point out at this interval that there are other regulations which a member must follow, but those regulations apply only to internal functions of the Brown Berets and will not be included here by order of Organizational Policy. c/s

# THROUGH BROWN EYES

An article by Lydia Perez, member of the Dallas Brown Berets, which was taken from La Onda Chicana, gives a perspective I feel is good to share at this point.

"Las Br own Berets

The Dallas Brown Berets (Las Boinas Cafe) were organized in 1969. Women Berets have been in Dallas as long as the male Berets, struggling for La Causa. We do just about the same things, and have the same opportunities that male members have in different activities.

We collect clothes, furniture, items from the people who donate to El Grupo, we also cook food as the men do for fund raisers to raise money for our Organization.

We also hold security for marchas, sell ads and write articles for La Onda Chicana, and are ready to fight, con our carnales, por los derechos de La Raza.

It doesn't matter if you are a man, woman, old, or young. We all have the same feelings, to educate and direct Nuestra Raza to the right sources when they need help. We need to let Nuestra Raza look out for themselves. We can't depend on agencies that are supposed to be helpful, or even the police for protection. You call the police for help and you turn out to be the victim in the hands of the law.

Women Berets love and respect all Chicanas and Chicanos, not because we are Berets, but because somos toda una familia of the same Raza. The Chicana has to protect ourselves and our children, also teach them to love and respect each other and La Raza.

We, the women Berets in Dallas, somos de diferentes ages. We are married and single. Some of us are working and going to college for a better education. Some of us have children. In addition the Brown Berets owe a great deal to the Chicanas that help nuestro Grupo, even though they are not members, they do much to help La Raza in their own way.

Carnalas out there, if you are reading this article, as you can see, it doesn't matter who or how old you are to want to help Nuestra Raza.

QUE VIVAN LAS CHICANAS!"

Finally, I think this following poem can also give you a Chicana point of view.

## CHICANA

As I struggle to survive

in a world filled with

hardships,

    disappointments

and delusions,

I see the face of my
mama,

and I feel her loving
hands

caressing me

en las mañanas

when she made me
my trencitas.

As I struggle through

roles I cannot endure,

woman,

Chicana,

mother, wife,

I see the gnarled,
swollen

hands of my mama,

quietly making

her tortillas

trempanito    en    la
mañana.

As    I    struggle    to
understand

to seek answers to

fill the voids,

the needs

in my life,

I feel the strength of
my mama

cuando se iba al fil

y en la noche

volvia cansada

a mas trabajo.

and from the images

of the strength of my
raices

I feel,

I am,

Chicana,

# THROUGH BROWN EYES

and will continue to
survive.

By Dannette S.Jacquez

This poem was taken from TIERRA Y
LIBERTAD, Enero 1980

Viva La Mujer!

# THROUGH BROWN EYES

## Chapter Five

## THE DALLAS BROWN BERETS

    I joined the Brown Berets in the summer of 1970, and joining the Berets back then was quite different from today. A friend and I went to the Brown Berets Headquarters, which was located at 42142 Sylvester. The Berets had a "Club House" (a garage) next to Kiko's Grocery. We went to the store and asked for the Brown

Berets. Ricardo Medrano introduced himself as the President of the Brown Berets.

We explained that we wanted to join, so he asked us a few questions, gave us some literature, and provided us each with a beret. We were in.

I had been interested in the Berets since seeing them in a march on television.

They seem to be the type of group which was not beyond my type of comprehension, was grassroots and was Movement oriented.

The Brown Berets turned out to be different from what I initially perceived.

Though they were involved in some Chicano-oriented issues, the Berets were used mostly for distributing Medrano campaign literature, bumper stickers, buttons, etc.

On March 02, 1972, the edition of the Dallas Morning News, a newspaper which is published daily in Dallas, Texas, contained an article by reporter Terry Klierwer entitled "Sit-In Staged By Youths at DCA Facility." It read as follows:

"Demanding the release of frozen funds for a poverty youth program, a dozen-or-so Mexican-American youths continued their day-long sit-in protest late Wednesday night at Dallas Community Action agency headquarters, 2000 N. Central Expressway, vowing to stay all night.

"The group sidestepped possible police intervention when DCA Youth Development Program Director Dick Hughes agreed to "work late" to allow them to remain in the building past closing time.

# THROUGH BROWN EYES

"Deputy Police Chief Paul Townsend appeared at DCA headquarters briefly to talk with DCA Interim Director Buck Johnson, to whom the youths' protests had initially been directed.

"Johnson told them he has no control over the frozen funds and pointed them to the 13-member Dallas County Youth Development Program board.

"Eight uniformed officers left the scene when Townsend departed about 8:30 pm.

"The youths were only part of some 45 students cut off from a total of $19,487 in education funds this semester when the YDP board of Directors froze the money Jan. 17.

"Hughes said the board's action also slapped a hold on about $20,000 in funds allocated for work training and recreation programs.

"He charged DCA board members Romie Lilly and Arthur Graves, who he said championed the YDP funds freeze, with 'featherbedding and pork-barreling.

"He said the pair joined YDP board President Judy Lewis Jan. 17 in persuading the YDP board to freeze $80,000 in funds for existing youth programs and divert the money into 'their own projects'."

A report from the Intelligence Section of the Dallas Police Department to the FBI, dated March 02, 1972, details in part that "On March 01, 1972, approximately fifteen Mexican-American youths who identified themselves to investigating officers as members of the 'Brown Berets,' Dallas, Texas, staged a sit-in protest at the Dallas Community Action headquarters (DCA)..."

The report went on to tell of the results in the sit-in: On "March 02, 1972, the DCA committee agreed to release approximately

$20,000 in educational funds for work training and recreation programs for students provided by the OEO through the Dallas Youth Committee and issued vouchers to the Mexican-American youths who were engaged in the sit-in demonstration at the agency's headquarters."

From the time I joined until about 1974, the Berets suffered with a generally negative image. One lady confronted a member and myself saying that she could not think of anything that the Brown Berets had ever done to help the community, and furthermore, that all the members were nothing but drunks, marijuana smokers, and criminals who were used by the Medranos to attack political opponents.

Though I wouldn't be able to account for the actions of the entire membership, I was perplexed by these actions and statements from a Chicana. I wanted to believe that the Brown Berets were really serving the Chicano Community.

We had just ended a 30 hour sit-in at the Dallas County Community Action Agency's Executive Director's office in conjunction with El Centro College students who had not received some tuition money promised by the Community Action Program. This was in March, 1972, the first and second days.

About the same time the National Brown Berets were having some internal problems. It seems that David Sanchez, then 214 and one of the founders of the Brown Berets, had been "straining his authority" and was strongly reprimanded by the Organization. Apparently his only response was to announce the alleged "disbanding" of the Berets. Referring to a "dangerous situation", on which he would not elaborate, he said, "It is time to go into a new phase of organization. All legitimate and official capacities of the Brown Berets National Organization have been dissolved. As Prime Minister of the Brown Berets National Organization and founder of the Brown Berets, I resign my post, as well as my membership." The only thing he accomplished was that the Brown Berets separated into state organizations, as well as individual local chapters and/or groups. But, the Brown Berets lived on.

In Dallas the Berets were going through their own internal problems. Some members wanted to continue working mostly on distributing Medrano campaign literature and the like. Others felt that there had to be more direct involvement in the Chicano Community and that the Organization needed to take on a service-oriented posture.

A variety of events had occurred by early 1974, which in my opinion, led to concern among many members here in Dallas about the direction of the Brown Berets locally. Along with Sanchez' "disbanding" of the Organization, which was on-the-whole ignored by the Brown Berets, another event which caught the attention of Chicano activists was the Chicano-police "battle" in Denver, Colorado. Chicanos in that city had for some time been having problems with the police. On March 17, 1973, Chicanos and police had a three-and-a-half hour gun battle. It seems, according to witnesses, that Luis Martinez was shot point-blank by the police as he approached the squad car to ask the police why they had shown up at the party.

The ensuing 3 1/2-hour battle resulted from the Chicanos choosing to physically defend themselves and not submit to oppression.

A slogan on the outside wall of the apartment of the party, which was bombed by the police, reads "Luis, we are not beaten, and we do not intend to be beaten or driven as such...what has happened here is but the sound before the fury of those who are oppressed!"

# THROUGH BROWN EYES

From late 1973 to about the summer of 1974, members of the Dallas Brown Berets headed out in all directions to get to know the Movement. Some went to California, some to Nuevo Mexico, others to Arizona, and still others to Colorado.

We wanted and needed to know Aztlan. But Tejas was different. We traveled throughout this state to visit all cities in which Berets existed.

My journey took me to several places. The visit I hold most dearly was the one to Pueblo, Colorado. Actually, I arrived in Denver first. Brown Beret member Josue Guevara went with me on this trip. He and I stuck together as far as Denver, and then he headed out to San Jose, Califas.

In Denver I accomplished one of my goals, which was to meet, spend time with, and be of service to Rodolfo "Corky" Gonzales.

It was also in Denver that I met the Pueblo Brown Berets. This group was the one I spent most time with. The first day in Pueblo, after driving from Denver to Pueblo with Eddie Montour and two other local Beret members, we drove straight to a house where I saw people picking up trash, painting, raking, piling wood, laying cement, and more. They were cleaning and repairing a house belonging to an older couple. They (the Berets) explained that every so often they select an older couple who is unable to make repairs, and then help restore the home and yard. Of course, being a nonprofit Organization, the Berets did the best possible with the money and resources available. Nevertheless, when we arrived at the home, I was promptly put to work alongside the others who also occupied the car.

Another incident which I will briefly touch on was a picket line held in front of the "minority" Councilman's house. Councilman Tekaki, the local "representative" of the minority community, had, according to the local Brown Berets, been voting on issues contrarily to the benefit of the community. At this demonstration, I learned the following song:

"No more Tekaki, (the space used by the Councilman's name can be substituted with any other) no more Tekaki, no more Tekaki over me, over me, oh before I'll be a slave, I'll be buried in my grave, and go home to Aztlan and be free."

During the summer of 1974, we started arriving from our trips. I was among the first of those returning to Dallas. As we started talking about our experiences on the road, and comparing notes, we started getting a better picture of how the Movement was supposed to work. We had learned the importance of Carnalizmo, Chicanizmo, Nationalism, and our Heritage.

Our first real action after returning was to confront the then Prime Minister, Ricardo Medrano, with our findings and conclusions from our experiences through-out Aztlan. We asserted that he was not applying himself to the Movement and was not directing the Organization accordingly.

It was during a meeting specifically called to discuss the above points that the part of the group wanting to change the direction of the Organization implemented a coup d'tat (an overthrow of power) removing those who wanted to continue with the same activities.

Ricardo Medrano, who was determined to continue as Prime Minister of the Berets, and who was also one of the ousted members, asserted that our coup would not be recognized and that they would continue as Brown Berets. We weren't too concerned about the challenge because it did not matter how many groups called themselves Brown Berets. La Raza would know us by our actions and not by any assertions.

The fall of 1974 found us eager for the upcoming years.

LEDBETTER, a barrio located in West Dallas, "came of Movement age." A group of 40 vatos met with me at the West Dallas Neighborhood Center to discuss the possibility of their organizing and becoming involved in the Movement. After a couple of hours of discussion, they decided to name themselves the Ledbetter Brown Berets.

Their primary effort concerned the Gabe P. Allen Elementary School (known to many Dallas residents as Emiliano Zapata). The Community decided that the school, whose population of Chicanos has always been over 95%, should have a Spanish name. The Ledbetter Berets had a meeting in that barrio at which those in attendance, made up of grassroots Chicanos from the area, voted unanimously to submit a list of names to the Dallas School Board for consideration. The list contained the names of many well-known persons, including Lorenzo De Zavala,

Erasmo Seguin, Emiliano Zapata and others.

The School Board quickly picked up on the name of Emiliano Zapata. He had allegedly been an "outlaw" and they could not accept that name. The Ledbetter

# THROUGH BROWN EYES

Berets then questioned "What about the rest of the names? What's wrong with them?" The School Board, probably thinking that they had a trump card, responded that they would not consider the name of Emiliano Zapata because he was not a U. S. citizen.

This time it was the community which made itself heard. Hundreds of persons came from all the barrios, groups, organizations, and factions of the Chicano Community. One-by-one many individuals, including myself, went before the School Board to urge them to respect the wishes of the Community and vote in favor of the name-change. When the Board again brought up Zapata's lack of citizenship, Dr. Glenn Lendon, a Southern Methodist University professor, pointed out that Dallas had a school named after a traitor to the United States, Robert E. Lee Elementary. We wondered whether being a traitor was preferable to being a noncitizen, or was it just plain racism.

The School Board then responded that if they renamed the school after a Spanish-speaking person, it could be interpreted as discrimination because it would imply the school was for "Hispanic" only. "There are over one hundred schools that are named after Whites", another speaker said. "Can't that be interpreted as discrimination too? What's the difference?"

Finally, the Board attorney, Warren Whitman (offering legal advice which Board member Robert Medrano said was "uncalled for") suggested that renaming the school could be construed by the courts as an act of segregation in itself. The Board voted 4 to 3 to refuse the name-change; as usual, the votes were along racial lines. The refusal of the School Board led to many actions, including a walkout (from the above mentioned meeting) by many persons,

including over 30 members of the Brown Berets. Pickets were set up in front of the School Administration building, and an eleven mile march from "Emiliano Zapata" Elementary School to the Administration Building was held on October 26, 1974. The demonstrations continued into late November that year.

An article which appeared in the Dallas Morning News, titled "Brown Berets Parade Protests Name-Change Denial" by Doug Domeier, told about a march the Brown Berets organized on this issue.

"A group of Mexican-American men, women and children walked approximately seven miles Saturday to protest the Dallas School Board's failure to rename Gabe P. Allen Elementary School for Mexican Revolutionary leader Emiliano Zapata.

"Sponsored by the Brown Berets, an activist Mexican-American organization, the parade left the Allen school, at 5200 Nomas in far West Dallas, with 80 to 100 persons at 10:10 am.

"Going east on Singleton, the number of participants grew to 200 by the time the group, frequently shouting "Zapata!" and

"Chicano Power," reached the Continental Bridge over the Trinity River.

"The figure held steady through 1:40 p.m. when the marchers reached the Dallas Independent School District Administration Building at 3700 Ross.

"Taking 3 ½ hours to cover the distance, the parade was thought to be one of the longest protest marches in Dallas history.

"'We have drawn attention to injustice,' claimed Juan Perez, Prime Minister of the Berets' Central Chapter in Dallas, in remarks outside the school building.

"Members of the Brown Berets said they sought the name change to remind Mexican-Americans of their cultural heritage and instill community pride in the school which has a predominantly Mexican-American student body.

"The School Board turned down the request last Wednesday by a 4-3 vote (I might add for the readers, that the 4 who voted against the name-change were White and the three who voted in favor were two Blacks and a Brown - J MP).

"Parade participants carried a picture of Zapata at the head of the procession followed by the Mexican and American flags.

"Escorted by the Police, the marchers stopped only briefly, for water or to let a funeral procession by. Several youths followed on bikes, as well as Mexican-Americans in cars.

"One Beret member said the group is talking with lawyers, considering filing a class action suit against the school board, charging contempt of U. S. Dist. Judge Sarah Hughes' June 5 order to correct institutional racism in the schools. It "The Berets may sponsor another march here Nov. 12, another member said.

Saturday's parade included Beret members from Austin, Houston, McAllen, and San Antonio, as well as Dallas."

The end of 1974 also heralded the end of the Ledbetter Brown Berets. The group, for reasons I will choose not to mention, disbanded. c/s

# THROUGH BROWN EYES

## THE NEW CHICANO

I Am The New Chicano.

I Have No Need For You,

Or Your Ways.

Nor, Do I Want To Be Like You.


You Have Sickened The Minds

Of My Carnales And Carnalas

With Hollow Promises,

False Hopes, And Lies.


You Have Made Them Ashamed

Of Our Culture, Our Language,

And Our Skins.


Yet!!!

You Offer Them Nothing Better.


And You,

You Are So Sick

And Infested With Your Diseases,

# THROUGH BROWN EYES

That You Can't Even See

Your Sickness

In Them.


I Am The New Chicano

El Mestizo, Hijo De La Raza

Soy Bronze, Hijo Del Quinto Sol.

And I Reject You.


I Want You To Leave My Country,

The Country You Killed And Murdered

My People For.

You Will Leave,

Or I

Will Drive You Off.

# *THROUGH BROWN EYES*

### Chapter Six

## THE YEAR OF THE BROWN BERETS

1975 began with the same negative tone with which 1974 had ended. Robert Ramirez, finding out that his dog "Ben" had fleas, tried to rid the dog of them. Being the poor man that he was, Ramirez used an old technique of rubbing grease on dogs and other assorted animals to smother, thus removing, fleas and the like from the creatures.

Unknown to Ramirez, who felt that he was doing no wrong in trying to help his dog, someone reported him to the Society for the Prevention of Cruelty to Animals (S.P.C.A.). For some reason (racism many of us believe), the S.P.C.A. pounced on this case with all for feet (sic). Ramirez was found guilty (?) and was sentenced to

THE DALLAS TIMES HERALD

POST-SENTENCE CONFERENCE — Robert ...... ..., probated, fined $250 and given a one-year probation center, chats with Brown Berets Juan Perez, left, and ... with numerous stipulations. He earlier had Victor Bonilla after he was sentenced to 60 days in ... been found guilty of cruelty to his St. Bernard, "Ben."

60 days in jail, probated, fined $250.00, and given a year probation term with numerous stipulations, including having to get his GED.

What this told us is that if you are found guilty of cruelty to animals (regardless of actual guilt) and happen to be of the wrong race, that you will have to do more than citizens of other races to "pay for your crime", including getting your GED. Racism acknowledges no boundaries but its own.

In February, we published the first and only issue of La Raza de Aztlan. The layout was awkward it was full of misspellings and very bad pictures, but it was the first. The paper itself became an object of conversation because it featured an expose of Anita Martinez's voting record as Councilwoman on the Dallas City Council. The facts, according to the paper, were not in Ms. Martinez' favor.

On Saturday, March 22, Mario Isaac and friends decided to have a get-together at a house in West Dallas. About 11:14 pm the police suddenly showed up at the gathering to find "several youths leaning against cars and drinking beer. One of the vehicles had its radio turned up loud." Any Chicano reading will quickly recognize that scene, as it is a common sight in any Chicano and poor community. One can go to any Chicano barrio on a Saturday night and find a group of youths leaning on cars, drinking beer, with someone's car radio playing loudly.

The police, who had yet to receive a complaint from any of the neighbors over the alleged noise, decided to put a stop to this. Their interference resulted in six more patrol cars being called out to the house, along with a helicopter and police brutality.

During the melee that followed, the police centered on Mario Isaac, then only 19 years of age, and started beating him, according to Mrs. Steven Mares, wife of one of the arrested men. Isaac's fiancée, Maggie Mares, said that she helped Mario into the house "because he was bleeding." She added that "Four police came in after him. They busted the door open. They had Mario on the floor. They were pushing tables around. They dragged him outside and were hitting him on the head with a flashlight." Mrs. Steven Mares said that her husband tried to help Mario, and when he did, "the police began beating him up. They came back after Steven after they put Mario in the car. They were beating Steven with a club. "The four officers who beat Isaac and Mares with clubs and flashlights were cleared by the police department.

As the Mario Isaac case was developing, another issue was coming into view. We had to postpone an "Unemployment March" so that the three organizations planning it could reorganize. The Brown Berets, the Black Panthers, and the Bois d'Arc Patriots decided to regroup before actually marching. We had attracted much attention, mainly because each group represented a different race, and we were working together. The Bois d'Arc Patriots is primarily made up of working class Whites. "Historically", one of the newspapers said, we should have ended up as "social, political, and economical enemies." Well, we fooled them. On Saturday, April 26, 1975, Dallas experienced its first tri-racially organized demonstration.

During this time the Berets kept hoping for a slowdown in activities so that some reorganization of the group could be initiated. One of the first changes that the group made was to dissolve the Prime Minister form of organizational structure.

Up until that time, I had been functioning as the "acting" Prime Minister. The Prime Minister form of organizational structure allows the "Jefe" (as Beret leaders are called) to exercise complete control over the Organization. David Sanchez and Ralph Ramirez, founders of the Brown Berets, selected this form of structure because it would allow the National Brown Berets to keep control of the entire Organization. Initially there was only one Prime Minister, David Sanchez.

Heads of the Chapters throughout Aztlan were all of the rank of Major. This meant that only Sanchez had actual control of the Organization. After Sanchez tried to dissolve the Berets in 1972, many Chapters decided to adopt the council form of organizational structure. This allowed the Chapters to appoint individuals to necessary positions (such as Minister of Information, Minister of Defense, Minister of Education, Minister of Treasury, and so on), and these officers collectively ran the Organization.

I was appointed Minister of Information. My duties included gathering information for, and distributing information about, the Brown Berets. I was given a rough draft of tentative guidelines for the position, and instructed to develop them into functioning guidelines for the Organization to consider adopting.

Along with the reorganizing, the Mario Isaac case, and the Unemployment March, the Berets became involved in what came to be known as "the Robert E. Lee issue."

In May '75, I received a call from Mrs. Susie Ramirez. She said that some of the parents of children from Robert E. Lee Elementary wanted to meet with the Berets concerning problems at the school. It seemed that complaints of abuse, and cruel and unusual punishment went back months, and, in some cases, years. One male teacher reportedly took "great pride in ruling his class with a leather belt which he... uses at will."

# THROUGH BROWN EYES

One child had "his head stuck into a trash can" for talking to another boy in line. Another parent told of "two Mexican-American children (in a classroom) sitting in a corner crying." The teacher explained to the visiting mother that the children "couldn't speak English and therefore she didn't know what to do with them as they were disrupting her class."

The parents pointed out to us how they had gone to other groups and places and couldn't find assistance. They were finally directed to the Brown Berets by others.

This case took us into April. There were many meetings. In most of these, Nolan Estes (then D.I.S.D. Superintendent of Schools) kept trying to "sweet talk" the parents. And even though he could calm them down some times, he could not break their determination to see this issue through.

On Monday, April 1it, the Berets assisted the families involved in this issue with a picket line. Beret involvement in the picket line was limited to monitoring the demonstration and informing the participants of laws concerning pickets.

Picketing the school turned out to be the focal point in this case. Up until then, the administration had been saying that they were not aware of any problems at the school. Mrs. Daria Valtierra explained why it took so long for their problems to be heard. "Most of us," she said, "believed that our problems could be solved by the principal, but when we would complain she would tell us not to worry about it because she would take care of it. We would never hear anything else about it. My little girl was slapped across the face after a tonsil operation - she still even had the stitches in her throat. She came home with a bad pain in her ear. The doctor said I should have called the police, but I made the mistake of telling the Principal. I finally decided to call the Tri-Ethnic Committee and the Brown Berets. Now I think we will get some action."

After the picket, the administration implemented an "investigation" and "inquiry" into the situation. A "Task Force" committee comprising six DISD employees (?) conducted the investigation.

The parents won it the end with the establishment of a Quiosco (a parent teacher meeting room), a Chicano teacher in every grade level, the replacement of the Principal and some teachers, and most importantly, DISD had been forced to deal directly with Chicano problems in the schools.

This was the year that representatives from all the Chapters got together in the small city of Edcouch, Texas. It was here that the many Chapters united under the umbrella of the LOS BROWN BERETS DE TEJAS, AZTLAN ORGANIZATION.

Becoming part of the statewide effort gave the Dallas Brown Berets a boost in morale. At this time there were many things happening that got us thinking more seriously about the future direction of our local organization.

# THROUGH BROWN EYES

On the fifth of May, the Houston police killed Jose Campos Torres. The following is a synopsis of the case by Los Brown Berets de Tejas, Aztlan Organization:

"Jose Campos Torres was arrested Cinco de Mayo at a neighborhood cantina in Houston, Texas for creating a disturbance. Six cops showed up to arrest Torres. Jose was taken to a secluded area known as the "hole" that is located right by Buffalo Bayou where five of the six cops made a semi-circle around Torres, cursing and beating him before taking him to be booked. Because Torres was so seriously injured, the jailer instructed the cops to take him to the hospital.

Instead of taking Torres to the hospital as ordered, the six cops returned to the "hole" where they beat Torres some more and threw him off a 16 foot embankment into the bayou. Torres' body was found floating in the bayou two days later on Mother's Day.

The six cops that were involved in the "murder" were Brinkmeyer, Kinney, Janish, Orlando, Denson, and Charles Elliot. Elliot, the rookie among them, came forward after the incident and admitted that he accompanied the rest of the cops to Buffalo Bayou and watched them push the badly beaten body of Jose Campos Torres into the bayou. 'Let's see if the wetback can swim' were the words that Elliot said he heard as one of the accused cops, Terry Denson, shoved Torres off the embankment.

People from everywhere were demanding that the six cops be indicted, convicted, and punished for MURDER. The trial was moved from Houston to Huntsville, 60 miles to the north, supposedly because of pre-trial publicity. But the people of Huntsville have the same radio and TV stations and get the same newspapers as the people in Houston. Furthermore, Huntsville is the home of the infamous Texas Department of Corrections, and the University there has one of the largest Criminal Justice

Departments around, which trains people to become cops, wardens, guards, etc. It is known to all Texas as a law enforcement town.

Of the 12 jurors who heard the cops: all were White; one person works as a prison guard; another was a former guard whose father is a highway patrol officer; the brother of a third juror is a campus police officer; and a fourth juror is a mechanic for the Huntsville Police Department.

Officers Brinkmeyer and Kinney were given state immunity in exchange for their testimony. Officer Elliot was neither charged nor fired from the police force. Janish was charged with a misdemeanor

From left, Juan Perez, Fred Bell and Charlie Young announce march postponemnt

and none of these cops came to trial. The two remaining officers, Orlando and Denson, were charged with murder. After a four-week-long trial, Orlando and Denson were found guilty of negligent homicide and given one year probated sentences and $1 fines for the beating and murder of Jose Campos Torres.

# THROUGH BROWN EYES

---

This incident is only one of a series of assaults that have ended up in the death of a victim. The intervention from the justice department has not prosecuted Darrell Cain, a police officer in Dallas who shot Santos Rodriguez a few years back."

One Chicano told me during this time that it seemed like open season on Chicanos. I thought about it... February 6, 1971, Alfonso Flores, killed, Pharr, Texas...

February 20,1971, Tomas and Berta Rodriguez, both shot, Dallas, Texas... July 22, 1972 Richard Joseph Lucero, beaten, Denver, Colorado... March 17, 1973, Luis Martinez, killed, Denver, Colorado... July 24, 1973, Santos Rodriguez, killed, Dallas, Texas... February 28, 1974, Raymond Montoya, beaten, Denver, Colorado... March 01, 1974, Virginia Gamboa, beaten, Dallas, Texas... April 19, 1974, Alberto Terrones, killed, Union City, California... July 04, 1974, Elisio Camargo, killed, Plainview, Texas... October 20, 1974, Richard Lopez, beaten, Albuquerque, New Mexico... November 01, 1974, David Gonzales, Lawrence Jackson, both beaten, Pueblo, Colorado... March 22, 1975, Mario Isaac, Steven Mares, both beaten, Dallas, Texas... June 13, 1975, Israel Rodriguez, killed, New York, New York... June 20, 1975, Modesto Rodriguez, beaten, Frio County, Texas... August, 1975, Alven Montoya, beaten, Albuquerque, New Mexico... September 14, 1975, Ricardo Morales, killed, Castroville, Texas... October 05, 1975, Richard Abeyta, Barbel Cruz, both shot, Central City, Colorado...November 09, 1975, Mrs. Toby Monreal, abused, Bellmead, Texas... You know, it did seem like open season on CHICANOS!

## ¿QUE SIENTO POR MI RAZA?

¿Que Siento Por Mi Raza?

Si No El Sufrimiento

De No Ser Educado,

Y De, Mas La Desgracia

De No Ser Unido.

Y Peor La Vergüenza

De No Defenderme

Cuando Me Golpean O Me Matan!

---

## *Chapter Seven*

## *INTERNAL REORGANIZATION*

1976 found us busily at work with our internal reorganization in its final stages. Locally the Berets had completed the first handout to distribute to the public to tell about the Organization.

I included it in its entire context:

"1976

The Brown Berets is an activist, Chicano, social service organization.

The purpose of the Berets is to provide assistance to Chicanos who have been treated unjustly.

LOCAL GOALS

1) To provide the Chicano community with a forum through which to voice their concerns.

2) To establish political education classes for the community.

3) To establish community rap sessions.

4) To encourage the community to demand that the Police Chief's position be made an elected one.

5) To establish a Citizen's Review Board of police actions, with members to be elected from the community.

6) To establish a Student's Rights Committee.

7) To provide inexpensive income tax preparation lessons and service.

---

QUALIFICATIONS FOR MEMBERSHIP

1) The applicant must be willing to do whatever work is required.

2) The approval of the unanimous vote of the members is required.

3) All new persons will be considered as Honorary until final approval.

LA FAMILIA CONCEPT

# THROUGH BROWN EYES

The family is the most important unit of the movement. Should any activity conflict with the welfare of the family, the family situation will be priority.

As the only thing more important than the Movement, La Familia Concept will be used as a guideline for attendance of members to Brown Berets functions.

REGULATIONS

1) A Brown Beret will always demonstrate self-discipline.

2) A Brown Beret will respect the beret itself, for it represents La Raza, Unity, Carnalismo, and the Organization.

3) A Brown Beret will never fight with another Brown Beret or a Chicano, except in self-defense.

4) No Brown Beret will indulge in narcotics.

5) A Brown Beret will always preach and demonstrate Carnalismo.

6) As Brown Berets we cannot fail to participate in any Beret activity unless it interferes with La Familia Concept.

7) No drinking of alcohol with the beret on.

8) These rules were not meant to be broken. Any member who persists in breaking these rules will be dealt with in the following manner:

First Offense: Reprimand

Second Offense: One Month Probation

Third Offense: Expulsion

9) A Brown Beret on probation may not wear the uniform."

This will show the reader the difference between, for example, joining the Brown Berets in 1970 as compared to 1976. Also, by the middle of the year, the Berets clarified a nine-point program. This I have included here also:

"NINE-POINT PROGRAM - DALLAS BROWN BERETS

1) We will work for the unity of all our people, regardless of age, income, or political philosophy.

2) We demand the right to bilingual education as guaranteed under the Treaty of Guadalupe Hidalgo.

3) We demand a Citizen's Review Board, made up of people who live in our community, to screen all police officers before they are assigned to our communities; and to investigate any police related complaints.

4) We demand that the true history of the Chicano be taught in all schools in the five (5) southwest states.

5) We demand that all police officers in the Chicano community must live in those areas and speak Spanish.

6) We demand that all Chicanos be tried by juries consisting of only Chicanos.

7) We demand the right to keep and bear arms to defend our communities against racist police as guaranteed under the second amendment of the United States Constitution.

8) We demand an end to all oppression, racism and injustice inflicted on people because of their race, color, creed, sex, or national origin.

9) We demand the right of self-determination within our community, leading to the eventual liberation of Aztlan."

The differences in this platform and the position that the Berets took in 1980 when they released for publication the "MANIFESTO OF LOS BROWN BERETS DE TEJAS AZTLAN ORGANIZATION." I have included it in its entirety:

Where-as, we believe that our home land has been invaded, COLONIZED, and raped; and where-as our Chicano People have suffered rather than benefited from all the personal loss, sweat and labor which built the Southwest, let it be known that:

We are the Brown Berets. We are a collective. Together we are a Chicano family that chooses to be a VANGUARD in our struggle for SELF-DETERMINATION. We believe that liberation can only be obtained when we have economical, sociological, and political control over our own lives. We have the right and ability to exist as an independent nation. We have our own culture, our language, and our own geographical identity.

We organize our barrios to proclaim our right to the soil; our own homeland. We organize our barrios at the local level because we believe that it is part of the process to obtain liberation for our nation Aztlan.

We have the right to own the land we work; our land is now occupied. The present occupation of the Southwest was not by treaty, annexation or purchase as we have been told by the Treaty of Guadalupe Hidalgo of 18148. But, let it be known for historical record that in 18146, Brigadier General Stephen Kearny, along with other U.S. forces, took possession of the Southwest by force. To prevent further battles between Anglos and Mexicanos who fought against the occupation at the time, a treaty was resolved in 18148 which was to guarantee rights to those (Mexicanos) who remained in the Southwest. President Polk, of the U. S., did not negotiate or process the Treaty of Guadalupe Hidalgo according to the U. S.'s own constitutional presidential powers. Technically, we are still in a state of war and our struggle against invasion and occupation exists, as it has since 18146.

Many of our people are imprisoned as political prisoners. The rest are imprisoned for violating laws we had no vote in writing in the first place.

We unite and work under the concept of Nationalism. Only GRASSROOT CHICANOS may speak for La Raza. Our first priority and responsibility is to our Chicano nation, wherever we are. We resist beccomming reactionaries—we struggle for self-determination rather than just react to crisis.

As an Organization we endorse no political party.

We support the masses against IMPERIALISM and their struggle for self-determination.

We are anti-CAPITALIST and are against personal profit or political gain from the liberation struggle.

REPRESSION

We must dismantle the police state. Through repression we are forced to submit to unwanted conditions and situations in our lives.

The unity of our race is the most important objective in our movement of resistance against the oppressive, capitalistic, and imperialistic system of the United States.

COMMUNITY CONTROL

Community control is to have control of our land, resources, and institutions.

EDUCATION

# THROUGH BROWN EYES

We must establish revolutionary free—schools. We must take control of existing schools in our barrios to insure proper bi-lingual education and cultural orientation.

For our pride and self-esteem, we want our schools named after our revolutionary leaders that represent liberation of Aztlan.

## MEDICINE

We must establish our own free-clinics to be controlled and operated by Grassroots Chicanos. We must expose and deal with hospitals that use our tax money on Band-Aid programs.

## COMMUNICATIONS

Mass media systems must be available for our people to use. We demand access to public media. We must establish our own public media. Community-controlled newspapers and teatros are vital in our movement. We must distribute and present PROPAGANDA.

We must demonstrate and protest in public institutions.

## FREEDOM

We must determine our own destinies and the future of our resources.

We demand freedom for all Latino political prisoners, including those being wasted for committing "crimes" against the capitalist system.

We support free travel throughout the Americas, without visas or passports for Nuestra Raza.

WE ARE THE BROWN BERETS. WE PROCLAIM TO NUESTRA COMMUNIDAD THAT WE STRUGGLE AND DIE ON OUR FEET, RATHER THAN LIVE ON OUR KNEESI

I have also included the definitions to many terms used in the Manifesto, as defined by the Los Brown Berets de Tejas, Aztlan:

**Manifesto** - way to tell the public who we are, what we stand for, and what we believe in.

**Colonization** - This is the result of the invasion and control, by outsiders, of our lives and our land.

**Vanguard** - Those leading the movement. The front line.

**Self-determination**     The right of Nuestra Raza to make their own political, economical, and sociological decisions.

**Nationalism** - A belief in Nuestra Raza and our nation. "Mi Raza Primero"

**Grassroots Chicanos** - Chicanos that live within the barrios and work towards and believe in the right to self-determination at no self-profit or self-political gain.

**Imperialism** - The action of spreading capitalist control in the U. S. over land and resources to maintain oppression through military (police) and economical force.

**Capitalism** - A system in which the rich are supported by the sweat and blood of the people.

**Repression** - Forces used to keep to people oppressed (such as through racist institutions like the police force, the education system and through capitalistic institutions like the banks).

**Oppression** - The conquered and suffering state in which we find ourselves.

**Propaganda** - A way in which to spread our beliefs and ideas. For instance our community newspaper is propaganda.

**Economics** - The way to achieve community control is to control the economy and the politics of the barrio.

**Socialism** - A system of social organization in which the producers (the workers) possess both political power and distribution means. It is the best form of economics that will benefit the common good for all people.

**Aztlan** - Physically, the five Southwest states - California, Tejas, Arizona, Colorado, and Nuevo Mexico.

Philosophically, the spirit of Aztlan is wherever there exists oppressed Chicano People; where we live is Aztlan, not the U. S. Un reconocimiento que todos Chicanos pertenecemos a una sola nación. No a la nación que han definido los "gringos." Aztlan es Nacionalismo.

Of course reorganization was not the only thing on our minds...

February 29, 1976, Pablo Garza, beaten, Bexar County, Texas... April 10, 1976, James and Robert Montoya, killed, Roger Montoya, shot, Albuquerque, New Mexico... May 5, 1976, Dennis Lucero, killed, Denver, Colorado... June 11, 1976, Barlow Benavides, killed, Oakland, California... September, 1976, Larry Corriz, shot, Antonio Devargas, beaten, Rio Arriba County, California... December 28, 1976, Datre White, beaten, Waco, Texas... When will it end?

I wonder often whether the police realize it or not that every time they commit is another atrocity, they only reinforce the growing opinion that the "law" is not for La Raza. They kill and beat our people, then they wonder why some of us are afraid of their law, and why some of us hate the nearness of the police.

# THROUGH BROWN EYES

## CHICANO

Chicano Is The Beginning Of Freedom,
And The End Of Oppression.

Chicano Is Self-Education.
Education Of The People, La Santa Raza!

Chicano Is The Child,
"Mexican American" By Birth, Chicano By Choice.

Chicano Is El Mejicanito,
Who Lives In Hunger, Because Of Prejudice.

Chicano Is La Mexicanita,
The Future Mother Of La Raza!

Chicano Is El Mejico-Americano,
Confused By Lies, Now Proud. Aware!

Chicano Is El Chicano,
Defending Life, Language, Culture.
Chicano Is La Causa!

# *THROUGH BROWN EYES*

---

Even At The Cost Of Death! Viva La Causa!

Chicano Is La Chicana,
Beautiful, Brave, The Seed Of La Raza!

Chicano Is La Raza Cosmica!
Born Of The Inequities Of A Government.

Chicano Is Pride,
Knowing Who You Are. Why You Exist.

Chicano Is A Language
Beautiful, Romantic, And Mine,

Chicano Is A Culture,
Tacos, Zapata, Cumbias, Aztlan!

Chicano Is My Son,
Born Of La Raza! To Die For La Raza!

Chicano Is My Daughter,
Born Of La Raza! To Live For La Raza!

Chicano Is My Brother,

---

# THROUGH BROWN EYES

Like Me, With Me, Y Mi Gente. Que Viva!

Chicano Is My Sister,

Who Loves Me, Cares For Me, Is Me, Together.

Chicano Is My Father,

Of Whom I Was Born, For Whom I'll Die.

Chicano Is My Mother,

Who Gave Me Birth, Life, And Reason.

Chicano Is My Wife,

I Love Her. She Is Always With Me.

Chicano Is Me,

A Man, Proud, Able To Choose And Live As I Want.

Chicano Is Chicano

# THROUGH BROWN EYES

# THROUGH BROWN EYES

## Chapter Eight

## A TIME FOR JUSTICE

On January 29, 1977, the Waco Brown Berets sponsored a "March for Justice" in the case of David Navarro. A leaflet by the Brown Berets explains:

"According to Coroner, Judge Joe Johnson, David Navarro did not die from stab wounds on his right arm August 11, 1976. The doctor who did the autopsy and Judge Johnson say David died from "natural causes". Three days after being taken to the emergency room for stab wounds, the Navarro family again tried to get David hospitalized for treatment and observation through a doctor who kept trying to delay it for a few more days. This was the same doctor on call who delayed hospitalization three days before. The doctor knew the family had no hospitalization insurance and was in no hurry to hospitalize David though he was in misery and pain with a swollen arm. Instead David was sent home with medication. With no apology to the family, the doctor, the corner, and another doctor who did the autopsy, are saying David died from Pulmonary Edema (fluid in the lungs). No X-rays were given David the night he was stabbed and no effort was made to justify how he was allowed to die. No explanation could justify how a boy so young could die from Pulmonary Edema.

This demonstration and rally will be aimed to expose the disgraceful system for hospitalization in Waco and how an unchallenged political system can cover up and protect those that run it."

# THROUGH BROWN EYES

The Randall Alan Webster case in Houston, was a real eye opener. After a highway chase of over 100 mph. speeds, police cornered "Randy" and forced him to stop. Eyewitnesses reported that when Webster stepped out of his van, police opened fire on him, killing the boy. Then one of the officers planted a "throw-down" gun (this is a gun which some police officers carry illegally to put on people they kill so that the officer can claim that he shot only in self-defense) to make it seem that Webster was armed all along.

Even after the officers involved were found guilty, they were only given one (1) Lear; each. The saddest thing though, was that the White community didn't even care. We finally realized that the "law" doesn't work even for the working class Whites, and that the White community, in general, doesn't care when one of their own is gunned down by the police in cold blood. But we knew, yes we knew, that it would happen again...

Cinco de Mayo, a time for celebration and a time for death... Officers who arrested Jose Campos Torres decided to beat him up a little. Later when the jail officials refused to accept the badly beaten Torres, the officers took him out to the Bayou, beat him up some more, and then decided to see if he could swim in that condition. His body was found floating in Buffalo Bayou three days later.

Three Houston officers: Terry Wayne Denson, 27; Stephen Orlando, 22; and Joseph Janish, 22, were found guilty of murder and sentenced to l0 years in prison, but me sentence was probated to five years(!?). This is justice??

When a Federal Appeals Court ordered U. S. District Judge, Ross Sterling, to imprison the three Houston police officers whose sentences he had suspended, the judge(?) responded by sentencing them to one year each. When the court of appeals ordered Sterling to give the officers more time, the "judge" added one more day to the sentences. JUSTICE OR JUST US?

As the Dallas Times Herald said on November 01, 1979, in an article titled "Myopic View of Justice", "In assessing three former Houston police officers the minimum sentence for their part in the 1977 drowning of Joe Campos Torres, U. S. District Judge Ross Sterling fulfilled the letter of the law, but trampled all over the spirit of it." But we knew, yes we knew, that it would happen again.

In Dallas, the Brown Berets, in conjunction with the Committee for Justice, Barrios Unidos, Bois d'Arc Patriots, Centro de Accion Chicano, Chicano Voters League, Committee for Positive Portrayal, FUERZA, La Familia, L.U.L.A.C. (state), Raza Unida, Refugio, and the South Dallas Information Center, started having planning sessions of our own on October 22, 1977, for a "March for Justice" in Dallas in November.

In Austin, the Brown Berets called a press conference on November 11, 1977, to denounce a serious case of police brutality and to answer questions on a "March for Justice" to be held in Austin the next day. In this case, 22-year-old Jesse and 21-year-old Johnny Maldonado suffered a serious beating at the hands of the "law" on November 0il, 1977.

# THROUGH BROWN EYES

The demonstration that we were planning in Dallas came off perfectly. Almost 300 persons attended the "March for Justice"

Paul Hernandez
Prime Minister
Austin Brown Berets

which started at 11:10 that morning. The main difference in this march and all others, is that this was a "silent" march. Marchers walked along quietly and somber "in respect for the dead."

On Tuesday, December 06, 1977, the U. S. Department of Justice announced that they were reopening the Santos Rodriguez case (this is the case in Dallas where Darrell Cain, a Dallas Police officer at the time, played "Russian Roulette" with a 12-year-old boy and fatally shot him in the head. He was eventually sentenced to five (5) years in prison and served only two-and-a-half (2 1/2) - JMP). Not only were we skeptical of this move, but we automatically assumed that it was only a ploy on part of the government to fool us.

Yes, in respect for the dead: 1977: January 19, Ruben Cortez, killed, Los Angeles, California... February 08, Randall Alan Webster, killed, Houston, Texas... February 14, Manuel Soto Flores, drowned, Mexican Border... February 20, Juan Zepeda, killed, Bexar County, Texas... February 28, David Dominguez, killed, Los Angeles, California... March 18, Carlos Duran, beaten, El Paso, Texas... March 20, Jesse Hernández, Adolfo Reyes, both beaten, San Fernando, California... April 03, Eduardo Prieto, beaten, El Paso, Texas... April 16, Edward Ramirez, killed, Los Angeles, California... May 05, Jose Campos Torres, beaten and drowned, Houston, Texas... May 05, Armando Montes, killed, Los Angeles, California... May 06, Ramon Longoria, drowned, El Paso,

# *THROUGH BROWN EYES*

Texas... May 14, Juan Veloz Zuniga, killed, Hudspeth County, Texas... June 02, Jose Roy Sanchez, killed, San Luis, Colorado... June Oil, Julio Osorio, Rafael Cruz, both killed, Chicago, Illinois... July, Jose Reyes, killed, Philadelphia, Pennsylvania... July 02, Jose Sinohui, killed, Tucson, Arizona... July 02, Salvador Muniz, beaten, Chicago, Illinois... July 14, Robert Max Moya, beaten, Albuquerque, New Mexico... July 30, Arthur Espinoza, James Hinojos, both killed, Denver, Colorado... August 15, Albert Zaragosa, beaten, San Antonio, Texas... August 20, Jose L. Davis, Daniel P. Hembree, both beaten, Albuquerque, New Mexico... August 22, Manuel Medina, killed, Seattle, Washington... August 26, Roberto Fernandez, killed Pueblo, Colorado... October 21, Noe Beltran, beaten, Ventura Flores, shot, Brownsville, Texas... October 29, Cresencio Ramirez, beaten, Waco, Texas... November 04, Johnny and Jesse Maldonado, both beaten, Austin, Texas... November 06, Tiburcio Santome, killed, Glasscock County, Texas... November 10, Andrew Ramirez, killed, Albuquerque, New Mexico... November 19, Chris Barreras, beaten, Albuquerque, New Mexico... December 09, Juan Galaviz, killed, Big Spring, Texas... Yes, we knew it would happen again, and again, and again...

Pura
Chicana

# THROUGH BROWN EYES

## Chapter Nine

## EL AÑO DEL CHICANO, PART I

Larry Ortega Lozano, a salesman, dies while in jail at the Ector County jail in Odessa, on January 22. The police claim the death was self-inflicted. Lozano had almost a hundred bruises throughout his body. The police claim he beat himself by running into the walls of his cell. Larry was held in a padded cell.

Brown Berets in Odessa, Big Spring, Midland, and Lubbock, began organizing activities around this issue, especially through a series of demonstrations.

Also on January 22, an El Paso County deputy shot and killed 15-year-old Danny Vasquez.

Pickets protested police brutality on January 24, 1978, in Houston, as the jury selection began for the federal court trial of four former Houston police officers charged with civil rights violations in the death of Jose Campos Torres.

In Austin, on February 05, the Brown Berets began a series of protests in conjunction with the East Austin barrio (E.A.S.T. Force) against the City of Austin's encroachment into the Chicano barrios. The demonstrations are centered upon boat races held in the East Austin area. Even though there were a few Chicanos who did not disagree with the races, most of the residents who showed their feelings were against the boat races because they created too much noise in their neighborhood. These races were held at times and locations (along the river close to the barrio) when the noise was most distracting to many of the residents.

On February 13, 1978, the West Texas Brown Berets called a press conference to announce a march to be held from Odessa to Big Spring, Texas. "The march," said Gilbert Herrera, Jefe of the Lubbock Brown Berets, "is specifically aimed at drawing federal attention to the death in Big Spring of 19-year-old Juan Galaviz, shot December 09, 1977, by Big Spring police as they perused an assault suspect.

Over 3,000 persons were involved in a demonstration against police brutality on February 19. The demonstrations, which included rallies in Midland and Odessa, were partially organized and implemented by the Brown Berets.

On February 25, 1978, the TEJAS BROWN BERETS ORGANIZATION held the march-caravan from Odessa to Big Spring with over one hundred and twenty-five (125) cars and over a thousand (1,000) persons participating.

One of the most unfortunate controversies to reach the public involving Brown Berets was the alleged resignation of Lubbock Jefe, Gilbert Herrera. Rumors had it that Herrera had problems with McAllen Jefe, Pablo Delgado. Another rumor had it that the Brown Berets were upset with Herrera for involving the Department of Justice's Community Relations Service.

But no matter what rumors are spread, the truth is that there was never any resignation or any attacks on one Beret member by another. The newspaper reports which were circulated on March 13, 1978, were false.

We really didn't have time to fight among ourselves anyway; it was on March 28, 1978, that the public received word through the media that "Judge" Ross Sterling had sentenced Jose Campos Torres' killers to just one (1) year in prison.

The Austin Brown Berets aided the Danny Vasquez Justice Committee, on March 31, in a picket line in front of the Federal Courthouse in Austin.

Nineteen individuals were arrested by the police on April 22, in Austin, during the demonstrations against the boat races. Allegedly, the police had told demonstrators that they had to stay on the curb - off the street during their demonstration at Lake Travis. One officer, according to a witness, "walked over to a pregnant woman and

grabbed her by the arm and started pulling her into the street." This action caused members of the Brown Berets and other demonstrators to come to the woman's aid, thereby violating the "stay off the streets" order by the police. The witness added, "Once the Berets and others were in the street, the police charged the demonstrators and began to attack aimlessly, with disregard for the facts of the situation. This action by the police resulted in suspension for a number of officers.

Meanwhile, two members of the Brown Berets, who were arrested the nineteenth, were conducting a hunger strike. The Berets refused to cooperate with the police and allow themselves to be fingerprinted and booked as though they had committed some crime. Supporters, as well as members of the Organization, held pickets outside the city jail until the release of the carnales.

By June of this year (1978), over half of the charges of "disobeying a lawful order" were dropped. May 08 - O9, 1978, hundreds of Chicano youth squared off against riot squad police in Houston. Rioting lasted a couple of days in that city. It seems that this is the only way that people can truly show their discontent so that it is not ignored.

# THROUGH BROWN EYES

While in Dallas we were busy with issues that never seemed to end, the Austin Brown Berets were also active. On April 22, 1978, 19 persons were arrested following a confrontation with Austin police at Festival Beach. Rain helped end the confrontation between police and 75 demonstrators, including members of the Brown Berets. No serious injuries were reported, except a policeman was hit over the head with a baseball bat, but his helmet took the force of the blow.

The confrontation started when, for some unexplained reason, police crossed the street to where the demonstrators were, grabbed a pregnant woman, and pulled her into the street struggling. The Brown Berets immediately went to her aid, "violating" a "stay off the street" order. Once the demonstrators were on the street, the police moved in to make arrests.

The Justice Department announced on May 14, 1978, that sixty (60) cases of police brutality against Chicanos, many involving local police, were under review by federal officials for possible civil rights violations. We took the news skeptically. How many times does someone have to lie to you before you know that they are liars?

# THROUGH BROWN EYES

The Tejas Brown Berets again flexed their muscles... On June 02, 1978, after months of planning, the Berets held a state-wide demonstration. Brown Berets in 20 cities simultaneously demonstrated. The 2-hour pickets, held at federal buildings throughout Texas, were organized to call attention to the rising police brutality problem. Some of the Chapters had to picket in the rain, but were not discouraged. In Dallas, we had about 50 persons, including Blacks and Whites, in front of the Earle Cabell Building. This was the same day the indictments were issued for the four Houston policemen involved in the shooting death of Randall Alan Webster. Still, we didn't believe anything real would come of it.

We try to be ready for the unexpected at any demonstration, but... The Austin Brown Berets put out a call for support to all Chapters for a march to be held in Austin on June 10, 1978. Representatives from many Chapters arrived in Austin for the event. The demonstration went well for the most part; it was against the boat races. It seems that the Austin City Council decided to hold boat races only in East Austin (in the Barrio), not in the White Community.

Staff Photo by Lon Cooper

Tom Laursa helps Juan Perez, hurt in the incident with the car. The driver was taken into custody but was not charged.

The Dallas Brown Berets sent ten members to Austin to assist in security (the Dallas Chapter is known for their ability in organizing very good security). The march was almost over when I received a "member needs assist" call over the walkie-talkies. I ran in the direction indicated by the member needing help. When I arrived at what seemed to be a clearing in the crowd, I stepped out just as a white car reached the place I was standing. It was moving fast. I instinctively curled up my right leg to absorb the impact I knew was coming. The car hit my leg and, I assume, because of the angle of my curled leg, it worked sort of like a spring, flinging me up and onto the front windshield. I was holding my walkie-talkie in my left hand. It caused the windshield to break and resulted in my left hand suffering a laceration.

The ensuing melee was predictable. After the speeding car caused me to roll over the top of the car and finally on the pavement, the other demonstrators attacked the car with clubs, sticks and more. The police finally cordoned off the car from the demonstrators.

I received a call the next Tuesday, in Dallas, from the Austin police, instructing me to be in Austin the same day at noon for the Grand Jury hearing on the incident. I received their call at 08:45 that morning. I told the officer that my left hand was completely swollen, I didn't have any money for gas, and anyway, I couldn't make it to Austin from Dallas in that little time. The officer said that he "sympathized", but that if I didn't show up to the Grand Jury they were going to drop all charges against the driver of the car...JUSTICE??

MUERTE A LOS VENDIDOS

Hector Flores and Rene Martinez turned out to be the first Mexican-Americans to be hung in effigy in Dallas. They (it was, and is still believed) were responsible in essence for Operation SER's being drastically reduced in funding, and for the city's eventual takeover of the program. Either Flores or Martinez, or both, was responsible for calling the investigation of SER which resulted in the program's eventual reduction in funds. This action hurt the program beyond control, and hurt the community it served irreparably. The people who hung them in effigy, which included the Brown Berets, were especially angry that they would even consider going to the city before trying to resolve the problems within our own. Sources indicated that Flores and Martinez took this step due to some disagreement between Martinez and the Program Director over the firing of Martinez' girlfriend for not doing her work correctly.

This action (hanging someone in effigy) was in itself a change in Chicano "politics." No longer will the VENDIDOS try the old "let's-not-fight-in-public-so-that-they won't-say-we-are-a-split-community" game. That mentality has been vanquished in Dallas forever. The vendidos will always be exposed and humiliated, whenever possible.

The newspaper today, June 23, 1978, said that "Justice Department officials have reached a tentative decision not to persecute a former Dallas police officer for his role in the 1973 killing of "12-year-old Santos Rodriguez. We could, and many did, predict these results. Oh well, it was just "tentative", right'?

On June 25th, another Chicano, Timoteo Rosales, is shot to death by officers in Plainview, Texas.

On June 28, 1978, the Brown Berets from Dallas and Joe Landin, then chairman of the Committee for Justice, attended the Dallas City Council meeting in an attempt to urge the Council to call for federal action in the case of Santos Rodriguez. Two Brown Berets and I held up enlarged photos of Santos, with the fatal wound in his head, throughout most of the discussion.

But it was Councilman Bill Nicol that made the E news. Seldom, to make my point clearer, does a group like the Brown Berets get "free" publicity. On this date, the "Councilman" asserted (with a clarity which escapes the average person) that he resented the attempt of the Berets to "intimidate the Council by coming down here dressed as storm troopers to represent a defiance I do not believe exists in the community." He was referring to about a half a dozen members in the audience, wearing the traditional brown berets of the activist Chicano organization.

Nicol continued that it was wrong to "dredge up" an incident that was five years old. "I've not heard," he added, "a single member of the Mexican-American community thanking us for an atmosphere that is so much better today than it used to be." I remember thinking at the time that it was like somebody wanting you to thank them because they are beating you "so much" less.

When asked what reactions we had to the Councilman's remarks, I answered that, of course, since I was in the meeting I had not had time to get together with other members to formulate a response. "But one thing's for sure," I said "Councilman

Nicol's remarks clearly indicate the level of his intelligence. It also demonstrates that he has no real contact with a large part of his constituency."

The reaction throughout the Chicano community was united and widespread. On the following Saturday, Councilman Nicol met with representatives of various Chicano organizations and individuals. It was obvious that Nicol understood the magnitude of his statements; throughout the meeting Nicol was mostly quiet and listening to the many speakers. We (the Berets) did not know how to react to him. Some in the Organization felt that a verbal confrontation was called for. Others said we should boycott any meeting he was in attendance at. Others wanted to organize pickets at his home and during Council meetings for a short period. The majority, though, decided that we should respond to his "child" (like in Transcendental Meditation) with our "adult." Those of us at this meeting were careful not to "intimidate" the Councilman in any way.

Other persons in the Chicano community were meanwhile reacting to the remarks. "It is very disrespectful to downgrade and publicly humiliate a community interest group that will use the democratic process by appearing before the City Council," said Dallas School Board member Robert Medrano.

"I think Mr. Nicol's choice of words was very unfortunate," said Adelfa Callejo, a leading Chicana attorney, "for Mr. Nichol's information, probably the majority of the Mexican-American community supports the Brown Berets. They're responsible for conducting peaceful demonstrations, not riots. The Brown Berets are the ones who should be given thanks."

Charlie Young, coordinator of the Bois d' Arc Patriots, called the storm trooper remark "completely absurd. Somebody like Nicol ought to go out and spend some time in lower-income areas of the city and be exposed to what people do feel and do believe. It's certainly improper to be labeling people, besides the fact that storm troopers are on the other side of the fence- the Nazis. He doesn't even have that matched up right. Nicol is driving people away from working in a cooperative way with city hall. He's alienating people who want to work within the system."

At the next council meeting Nicol issued a statement apologizing for his choice of words. The press took this to mean that he was not apologizing for what he meant, just for his choice of words. "His personal feelings, or opinions, are totally unimportant to us," I said to them. "He has a right to his own opinion. It's his actions which concern us. We will hold no animosity toward Councilman Nicol."

...1978: January 22, Lorenzo Ortega Lozano, killed, Odessa, Texas... January 22, Danny Vasquez, killed, Moon City, Texas... January 01, Paul Martinez, killed, Perryton, Texas... April 04, Tony Garcia, beaten, Bill Amador, beaten, San Bernardino, California... June 18, Edgardo Ortiz, beaten, Philadelphia, Pennsylvania... June 25, Tim Rosales, killed, Hale Center, Texas... and the list goes on... and on...

## I WILL ENDURE

I Awaken.

I See Before Me A Vision.

I See Myself Attacked With Hate,

The Sword Of Racism Cuts Me.

Discrimination And Bigotry,

Trample Me To My Death,

I Am Hung,

I Am Beaten,

I Am Robbed,

I Am Killed,

I Am Dead.

Yet,

I Live...

I Live In The Most Desolate Of Places....

Alone.

# THROUGH BROWN EYES

I Search For Ways To
Help Myself

To Prove

Even If To Myself

That I Can

And Will Overcome All
Obstacles.

I Am Tired.

I Have Existed In An
Anglo World.

I Have Been Infested

With The Sickness Of
Hate And Prejudice

Of The Anglo Society,

But Yet,

I Have Endured,

And

I Will Endure.

# *THROUGH BROWN EYES*

## Chapter Ten

### EL ANO DEL CHICANO, PART II

Gilberto Herrera
Prime Minister
Lubbock Brown Berets

Juan M. Perez
Prime Minsiter
Dallas Brown Berets

Brown Berets from the Rio Grande Valley take over and occupy El Colegio Jacinto Trevino, consisting of 32 acres in San Juan, Tejas. The Berets held firm for forty-nine (49) days until Hidalgo County court ruled in favor of the Berets over "Corrupt Administrators."

And it was Thursday, July 13, 1978, that the Justice Department "formally asked that the 10-year suspended sentences given in the Jose Campos Torres case be re-imposed."

The Tejas Brown Berets once again were in the news with a protest march being held in Plainview, Texas on July 15. This "March for Justice" was for Tim Rosales and Juan Benito Martinez, who was killed on July 8, 1978, in Laredo, by patrolman Antonio L. Elizalde, Jr. 30, who said it was an accident. Surell At the demonstration there were, it was estimated, between 800 to 1,000 persons in attendance.

On the 15th of this month (July) the Justice Department dropped the Santos Rodriguez case. Then Attorney General Griffin Bell decided not to bring federal charges against Darrell Cain, Santos' killer, because "the state prosecution of Cain was prompt and vigorous and resulted in a jury conviction of the highest degree of murder and a jury-set jail sentence involving his imprisonment for a term of years."

Cain was convicted of "murder with malice" and sentenced to FIVE (5) years!!?? And then he only served 2 ½ years of the time!!!

"Texas Leads In Hispanic Rights Cases," read the headline of an article in the Lubbock Avalanche-Journal, July 16, 1978. "More than ninety (90) percent of the cases reported from Texas involve allegations of police brutality." It also quoted Dan Rinzel, a member of the Justice Department's Civil Rights Division, as saying "we certainly get more complaints from Texas than from anyplace else."

On the l6th of July, the Brown Berets and the Committee for Justice, under the leadership of Perfecto Delgado, held a long planned march for Santos Rodriguez. Three hundred persons attended the march, primarily Chicano, but also with Whites and Blacks. The march left Reverchon Park at 8:30 pm and walked down Maple to the 2200 block of Cedar Springs, where Santos Rodriguez was fatally shot.

Among the many cries for justice coming from the crowd one could constantly hear the shout "VIVA SANTOS!"

# *THROUGH BROWN EYES*

It was the 17th of July, 1978, that the Federal Grand Jury began hearing testimony from officers and witnesses about the arrest and jail death of Larry Ortea Lozano, a 27-year-old hotel supply salesman from Pecos. The Grand Jury was allegedly looking for some evidence of possible civil rights violations by officers involved.

On July 18, the Midland Brown Berets were also demonstrating. They demanded a federal probe into the killing of Larry Ortega Lozano. The Berets wanted the Federal Grand Jury to hand out indictments against Ector County officials.

"In Houston, today, a group calling itself Chicano Citizens in Action said July 21 it was making a phone number available for persons to report alleged cases of police brutality. The group was formed this past weekend as a result of what spokesperson Rachel Navarro said was a case of Police Brutality on the city's north side involving four Mexican-American," said the Dallas Morning News on July 7, 1978.

All around us the Movement was continuing and growing. Lubbock, Plainview, Odessa, Houston and Dallas. More people becoming conscious of La Causa and getting involved. Viva La Raza Siempre!

DALLAS. July 22. Three hundred people came out to march in what was to be the last march specifically on the Santos Rodriguez case. It will never be, though, the last time we call for Justice for him.

Brown Berets from all over the State of Texas attended the march to help with security. This march was well planned and coordinated, and included many organizations like the Committee for Justice, the Mexican American Assembly for Civic Involvement, Bois d'Arc Patriots, and others. The Greater Dallas Community Relations Commission also played a part. They provided 44 individuals, who were not part of the demonstration, from various local churches to be neutral observers for the march.

The Texas Sun, a newspaper from Corpus Christi, had an article in it, on July 31, 1978, which reported an interview with me concerning the Brown Berets. The article, titled "Aztlan Just a matter of time - BROWN BERETS WANT SEPARATE COUNTRY", is written by Bill Hendricks of the SUN staff. It served to give the public a perspective on the Brown Berets which was, in my opinion, very much needed. It also helped look at a member of the Organization from a human point of view. I have included it here in its entirety, to give you an opportunity to make your own judgement:

"DALLAS - Eventually much of what is now the Southwestern United States will be a separate country. It will be independent of the United States or any other nation. Political and economic power will be in the hands of a mostly Chicano group dedicated to the happiness of all it's (sic) people.

"That nation will be called 'Aztlan' and will consist of parts or all of the present states of Texas, New Mexico, Colorado, California, Utah, and Nevada.

"Far-fetched? Perhaps. But Juan Perez and other members of the Brown Berets organization claim it is what Perez calls a 'reality.'

# THROUGH BROWN EYES

"Perez describes the attainment of "Aztlan" as the long-range goal - an accomplishment he said is being proved possible every day by the failures of the system. 'My grandson probably will not live to see it,' Perez said, 'but it is a reality.'

Perez, 26, is the publicity coordinator for the Dallas Chapter of the Brown Berets, an organization that has been in the news recently for its feud with Councilman Bill Nicol and for the active role it played in demonstrations condemning the decision of the U. S. Justice Dept. not to prosecute a former policeman who shot to death 12-year-old Santos Rodriguez.

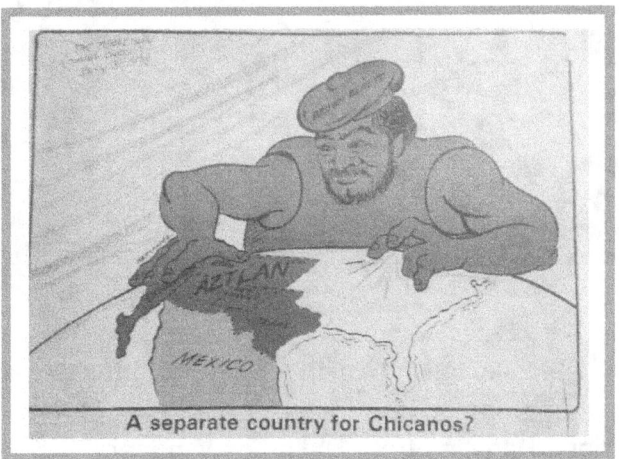

A separate country for Chicanos?

"The young Chicano is a student at El Centro College. He spends most of his time working for the Brown Berets cause. His wife works but he says he does not have a full-time job.

"'I am not ready to be exploited by the system,' he said. 'One day I will have to accept it but not right now.'

"Brown Berets, an organization that grew out of the formation in 1967 of the Young Chicanos for Community Action in Los Angeles, are growing - not just in numbers, but in political impact among Chicanos, Perez claims.

# *THROUGH BROWN EYES*

*"Why does it happen?" Perez asks, referring to police brutality to hispanics in America, documented in scrapbooks of newspaper clippings.*

"While talking to the SUN reporter, Perez sat a table in the living room of his tiny second-floor apartment. As he talked, he clipped articles from Dallas newspapers and fielded telephone calls concerning another demonstration to express Chicano outrage in the Rodriguez case.

"Perez is a bearded young man who appears even younger than he is. He describes the struggle towards "Aztlan" as more of a class undertaking than a racial one.

"It is, he said, a case of have-nots throwing off the shackles of "capitalistic oppression.

"Aztlan will be ruled under a system Perez called 'nationalism.'

"'The Brown Berets don't believe in communism,' he said, 'mostly because we don't understand it.'

"'Socialism in some ways fits our thinking, but nationalism is our goal.'

"Perez described 'nationalism' simply as 'the retaking of our homeland.'

"When considered in historical perspective, Perez said, the goal of Aztlan becomes more possible. He said it is the same thing the Jews did in Israel and French-speaking citizens of Quebec did in Canada.

"Perez sees a Brown tide sweeping the Southwest, with Chicanos gaining more and more political power.

"Already, he said, the results can be seen in the election of President Carter and John Hill's defeat of incumbent Gov. Dolph Briscoe.

"Chicano votes played a considerable part in the outcome of those two political campaigns, he said.

"In not to many years, Perez predicts, as the Chicano population grows toward a majority, Mexican Americans will control all the political machinery in the Southwest.

"He kept emphasizing that the goal of the Brown Berets is not merely to win control of the present system, but to change it to a political form that they feel will be more responsive to the people.

"Perez said that, at present, he is distrustful even of Chicano officials, because he feels they must serve the interest of the white establishment or they have no hope of winning elections.

# Marching To Aztlan

**BROWN BERETS**

"The only way the Brown Berets could see their dream of Aztlan fail to materialize is for the present political and economic system to extend its benefits equally for all, Perez said.

"But he added that this will never happen, and that as a result, the days of the capitalistic system are doomed.

"'Every time there is another Santos Rodriguez case - every time there is another incident of more oppression and injustice - we are proving our point,' he said.

"It is the failures of the system that will hasten the realization of Aztlan, he said.

"'You have to keep bringing up the issues,' he said. 'If everything was okay, why would we want to separate? But it is not okay.'

"When President Carter had announced that he had instructed Atty. Gen. Griffin Bell to review the Santos Rodriguez case, Perez said he went into the Mexican American community and said there would be no prosecution.

"'They told me I was wrong,' he said, 'They said Carter cared about them. But we see now that there is not going to be any prosecution.'

"Perez predicted more injustices and oppression, a continuation of a system that he said discriminates not just against Mexican Americans and Blacks, but against poor whites.

"This will not change, he said.

"'It is not going to happen,' he said, 'because it would mean we'd have power, and they are not going to let us have power.'

# THROUGH BROWN EYES

"At present, Perez concedes, the Brown Berets are relatively small in number, but he claims they are more active than most other groups.

"He bragged that they owe no one, unlike what he said of such Mexican American organizations as the American G. I. Forum and the League of (United - JMP) Latin American Citizens (LULAC).

"'All of our money comes from our pocket, or from a few people who believe in what we are doing,' Perez said.

"He said the Brown Berets don't care whether they lose their jobs.

"All their efforts, in a long range sense, are directed toward realizing Aztlan and its system of nationalism.

"'The system we have now doesn't even work for Anglos,' Perez said. 'They (the establishment) are going to keep playing games with us. They are going to keep using us. They still say, - This is bad, and that is bad - But they are not going to do anything about it. They will try to please us with words.'

"'Capitalism is bad, because it creates a small group of people who exploit a large group of people to keep their power.'

"But things will be different in Aztlan, he said. And to Juan Perez and the other Brown Berets, Aztlan is just a matter of time."

On July 25 a rally and march were held in Laredo protesting the recent shooting death of Jose Antonio Martinez by a Laredo policeman. Over 400 persons blocked the International Bridge to Mexico.

Over 400 people march in Kingsville on August 05, to protest the deaths of Gregorio Espino in a Kingsville jail in March '78, and Jesus Garza in Robstown.

# THROUGH BROWN EYES

One thing that seemed to be on everyone's mind in Dallas (sort of like the shooting of J. R.) was the Cullen Davis trail (at least during this time period). The August 23, Dallas Times Herald, page 4-A, had an article titled "Plan To Blame Killing on Brown Berets Claimed." It goes on to say "In a meeting early this month, McCrory said, Davis suggested two ways to kill Eidson and blame the killing on a Mexican-American group, the Brown Berets."

"Either way, Davis thought, it could be blamed on a Brown Beret because of the uprising. He said get a Mexican-American's driver license and cap and drop them at the scene...then send a tape to some TV station and let the Brown Berets take the blame for it, stated McCrory."

In another part of the paper "Now wipe that S.O.B., take the clip out and wipe it down, too. Now, the, uh, does it make any difference to you what color the silencer is or you just want one with a f ---- -- silencer period? The Brown Beret cap to drop by the Judge. S--- man, where do you find one of them mother f-----?

If you're going to blame it on the Brown Berets, where do, where in the f---, where do you find one of their caps'? There's not any."

The Brown Berets' response was "To attempt to blame our Organization for the murder of a divorce judge implies that we are something other than a community service organization. The Brown Berets in the past have never been involved in that kind of activity, and we don't intend to be involved in that kind of activity. In essence, we resent the plot to blame us."

The demonstrations in Austin were still going strong on August 12, when the East Austin community and the Brown Berets held their third demonstration in a series of activities aimed at stopping the boat races.

# THROUGH BROWN EYES

In August we found out about Jesus Martinez Gallegos. He had had family problems and left his house in Waco, Texas. A short time later he came back and forced his way back in. About the same time the police had arrived. They took one "witness'" comment about Gallegos' presence in the house to mean that a burglary had taken place and that Gallegos was the burglar.

Gallegos became frightened, ran, scuffled with an officer, broke free, and was shot to death. Some of the officers at the scene said that the policeman who shot Gallegos "overreacted." In any case, as the Dallas Times Herald said in their September 01, 1978, editorial on the incident, "Whatever the outcome, Gallegos' death simply hardens the conviction held by many Mexican-Americans that they are targeted people in a land of plenty. And, more often than not, they are right." And as if that wasn't bad enough, on August 29th, Rockwell County, Texas, deputies went to a farm house where there were supposed to be some undocumented workers. Circumstances occurred which led to the shooting of Coronado Munoz, 30. Inconsistencies in the reports filed by the "law enforcement" officers drew much attention. One of the

Juan Perez          Fred Bell          Charlie Young
Brown Berets      Black Panthers   Bois d"Arc Patriots

representatives of 17 groups, which got together to call for a federal investigation in the shooting, reported the incident to the United Nations' Human Rights Division. "How long is there going to be bloodshed at the hands of the police?" asked Eloy Zamora, a representative of the Mexican American Assembly for Civic Involvement, "How many more Mexicans are going to be killed? How many more hands and feet or whatever are going to be lost? (Coronado had to have his left foot amputated due to the shooting). It's got to stop."

Charlie Young, of the Bois d'Arc Patriots, said he was opposed to "the lack of accountability and sensitivity" on part of policemen. He added that the Patriots are "against anyone's civil rights being violated. But it seems to continue. It's particularly intense in the barrios."

Bill Stoner, representing the Uhuru Family, said "We constantly ask for police protection, but what we get is police brutality. I'm pleased that we are banding together all these organizations representing different ethnic groups to unite against police brutality."

Charlie Young and Bill Stoner are two of the people that the Dallas Brown Berets have the highest respect for.

We received a letter that month that I believe I should share with you, dear reader. It is typical of Brown Beret determination:

Start ---

"Querido Amigo, Juan, 09-08-78

I'd like to be of service, but my time, energies, and financial abilities are limited. Also, my past ventures with Chicano groups have been varied, rewarding but also disturbing to me. While I am not completely prepared to close the door on Chicano affairs, neither am I totally prepared to volunteer without limit.

# THROUGH BROWN EYES

As you see from the materials I am enclosing, I have had wide experience in publication (original poetry, professional articles in various magazines, articles on different subjects in newspapers around the country, and the newsletter I put together, doing: layout, photography, design, interviewing, writing, solicitation of funding).

I have also considerable experience in public relations, apart from my many years of university teaching. I have organized various groups and programs and have had wide contact with municipal, state, and federal contacts.

What I'd like to do is write a regular article or column for your newspaper. It must be free to touch on any subject even those you may not totally agree with-- otherwise it cannot be viewed as a "forum" as you promise in your first issue. I don't think I would clash with your general purpose, but I may have my peculiar ways of saying it, and my view and philosophy may go well beyond anything you may have had originally in mind--but it will still further your cause.

From this editorial base, we might move on to bigger and better things. However, I should make clear from the outset that I do not want to be a visible activist except through the column--which I may even write under a fictitious name if it doesn't clash with your policy. I want to be a resource person, a volunteer who gives in his own way, in his own time, in his own style. I don't expect to attend meetings or demonstrations, but I may under circumstances (determined by myself).

If you think you can use me under these or similar conditions, I'd like very much to help. I'll be happy to meet with you at your convenience (as much as possible)."

The writer's name I left out to protect the - uh – innocent?

Our reply to the letter was:

# *THROUGH BROWN EYES*

There are no members or supporters of the Brown Berets Organization who could (even if they wanted) "volunteer without limit." They are, though, determined to do their share in El Movimiento.

La Causa is like a giant machine, it requires many smaller parts to keep it going. These smaller parts, though they all perform different functions, have to always keep working at their fullest potential to keep the machine running. Should even one of the parts change its necessary function, or work only sometimes, then that part eventually becomes a hindrance.

We are impressed with your articles and obvious large resources of information you must have, but... We wish to put the word "forum" into its proper perspective. The Brown Berets are available to the Chicano community, as we mentioned in our paper La Onda Chicana, Page 2, "Brown Berets", Paragraph 3 in "The fields of Police Brutality, Job Discrimination, Education, Discrimination in General, and Inequality in Justice." Should any Chicano suffer these, we can, if the individual chooses, represent him (them) before any entity necessary. We also except people's opinions and channel them to the right agencies. We also support persons in their struggle when it is the same as ours. It is our forum for our community.

We have never, nor do we intend to, provide a forum for any person(s) who does (do) not see reality as we do. There are too many issues that need to be exposed, and too much useful information that needs to be disseminated to La Raza for us to consider allowing any articles in our newspaper which we "may not totally agree with."

We need people who understand the Cause, realize the need for the movement, and are prepared to dedicate their lives to our struggle. El Movimiento is not a part-time "job." We are not trying to prove anything. We realize the severity of this situation and the need for a solution.

A "volunteer who gives in his own way, his own time, in his own style" would be in conflict with our belief that a community which is educated, made conscious and organized, can be its own best defense against any type of oppression imposed upon it.

We thank you for your offer, but we have many good writers who can use newspaper space to promote La Causa and open minds.

Venceremos, Juan M. Perez"

End ---

The 9th of September found Weslaco, Tejas, in the center of a demonstration organized by the Brown Berets. Over 500 Chicanos attended a march protesting police brutality outside the Weslaco Police Department. The Police Chief is "forced" outside to hear demands for the resignation of city officials, as well as himself.

On the 13th of September, a Fort Worth police officer was suspended indefinitely without pay for allegedly beating two prisoners. Officer K. L. McCoy, according to Police Chief A. J. Brown, "struck a Mexican-American prisoner in the Fort Worth City Jail booking area several times in the head with his hands and

when the Mexican-American fell to the floor...Kicked him in the head several times."

Brown also said, "As a result of the unnecessary physical assault on the prisoner who was offering no resistance whatsoever, (the prisoner) lost so much blood from his injuries that other employees of the jail had to mop blood from the booking area floor and wall."

San Antonio. September 14, 1978. Demanding an end to police brutality, more than forty (40) persons marched from Elmendorf Park to Alamo Plaza to hear speakers. The rally after the march lasted Two-and-a-half (2 ½) hours.

The Brown Berets also organized a caravan (this is where cars are lined up along the road to show support or protest of an action or incident) and demonstration in Robstown, Tejas on September l6, which is also a Mexican Independence Day.

On the 22nd of September, representatives of the major Mexican-American and Chicano organizations, met with Chiefs of Police from throughout the state of Texas. Attendees included: (Yours truly) Juan M. Perez of the Brown Berets; Ruben Bonilla of the League of United Latin American Citizens; Representative Paul Moreno D-El Paso, Chairman of the Mexican-American Caucus; Jose Garcia of the Incorporated Mexican-American Employees; Jose Cano of the G. I. Forum; and Joaquin Avila of the Mexican-American Legal Defense and Education Fund. The Police Chiefs in attendance included: Donald Byrd of the Dallas Police Department; William Banner of the Corpus Christi Police Department; Frank Dyson of the Austin Police Department; Emil Peters of the San Antonio Police Department; and Andres Vega of the Brownsville Police Department.

Each person had his own reason for being there. The Brown Berets instructed me to respond in this manner: "My attendance in no way represents the Brown Berets official sanction of this meeting." My position there was to be an active observer, and to see that there would be no "hanky-panky."

This September the Berets decided to run a candidate for the Dallas City Council. The reasons were two-fold. First, we needed to expose some needs of the Chicano community and running for office always guarantees media exposure. Secondly, should we have decided that there was a real chance of winning, we wanted to provide voters with a choice which would not have sold out at any cost.

The Brown Berets believe that a person on the City Council should be totally responsive to the needs of the community, even to the point where the community gives her/him the direction to be followed; the community should dictate how the Councilperson votes.

4D  The Dallas Morning News   Thursday, September 7, 1978   ★★★★

# Hispanic plans council campaign

By BONNIE BRADSHAW

Juan Perez, a member of the Brown Berets, announced Wednesday he plans to run for Place 2 in the 1979 Dallas City Council elections.

"A month ago I would have told you that I'd never run for City Council," said Perez, public relations coordinator for the Brown Berets, a Mexican-American activist group. "But we decided that if we wanted someone who would be vocal for projects we wanted, we would have to run someone ourselves."

Incumbent Bill Nicol, who is not expected to seek re-election, has been described by Brown Berets as "insensitive" to the needs of Mexican-Americans in District 2, which includes West Dallas and north Oak Cliff.

School board member Robert Medrano, cautioning against splitting the Mexican-American vote in District 2, said Perez' announcement was premature.

bombards our plan of action."

Medrano said the assembly was planning a conference in late October to select a candidate who would have the unified support of the Mexican-American community in District 2.

But Adolph Canales, spokesman for the civic involvement assembly, said he wishes Perez the best of luck.

Canales said the main purpose of the conference planned for October is to assess the goals of the organization, not to talk politics.

"I'm sure politics will come up, but that was not the intent of the conference," Canales said.

Perez, who said he expects at least two more Mexican-Americans to enter the race, said a split could be avoided by holding a "primary" within the community.

Canales said holding a primary had not been discussed during a formal

Dallas News staff photo

Juan Perez . . . a "vocal" candidate.

Councilpersons should get out and actively meet the community, get to understand the various needs, views, and opinions of the members of her/his district, and base her/his vote on the general feelings of the community.

The Brown Berets' Platform read as follows:

1. An end to police brutality.

2. Promoting a neighborhood safety council.

3. Night City Council meetings to enable the day worker to become actively involved in city politics.

4. Improved city streets and health facilities.

5. Bi-lingual City Council meetings.

6. A Citizens' Review Board composed of citizens elected from the single member districts who would screen police officers before they are assigned to each district and would help investigate police-related complaints.

The Los Brown Berets de Tejas, Aztlan Organization held a caravan and march from McAllen to San Juan, Tejas on September 30. They hold a gun salute which is "heard throughout downtown Pharr," where Berets pay respects to Alfonso Laredo Flores who was shot to death in 1971 by a Department of Public Safety (ironic, huh?) officer.

Adan Hernandez is pronounced dead in Houston on October 28th, having been beaten and found hung in a Houston jail a week earlier. Rio Grande Brown Berets began an immediate investigation of the death of the native Mission, Tejas, Chicano. Justice Committees are organized in both Houston and Mission.

Parts of the Tejas Brown Berets, organize a demonstration in Moody Park in Houston during which members were armed for an

# THROUGH BROWN EYES

18 gun salute in commemoration of the 18 Chicanos which had died at the hands of the law to date.

About 7:30 pm on November 21, 1978, Mrs. Dolores Zamora called the police. She wanted them to hold her husband, Julio Zamora, Sr., whom she had been having a quarrel with, so that she could get her children in her car and go stay with an aunt.

While officers were at the residence, Mr. Zamora was outside with one of the officers. Zamora took out a cigarette and started smoking. The officer told him he couldn't smoke. Zamora answered that he was on his own yard and that he was not under arrest, therefore he continued to smoke. The officer then grabbed Zamora, who swung at the officer. The two started struggling and the other officer (who was inside all this time) came out to assist the first officer.

Ercilia Zarate

Mrs. Zamora and the children came out in time to see the both officers holding Zamora down and "Choking him." The children suddenly became frightened, ran to where their father was lying and tried to pull the officers' arms so that they would stop choking their father.

One of the officers turned around and swung his stick, striking Julio, 8, in the side. The officer made a grab for him, but little Julio turned and ran. The other officer turned and grabbed 12-year-old Carolyn Valderas by her hair and put a choke hold on her. The officer who struck little Julio, then grabbed Carolyn's hands, fractured her thumb, and handcuffed her.

Two weeks later (as in all cases of this kind) the Internal Affairs Division reported that a part of the complaint has been partially sustained (that's when they decide that the complainant was right). They said the officer had been found guilty of cussing!?

Carrying signs that read "Now they're after our children" and "Cockrell Hill needs justice", 50 demonstrators marched through the city of Cockrell Hill as the Brown Berets provided security. The march was to protest police brutality. The Zarate family said that officer James Baggett came to their house looking for the family's eight (8) year-old boy for allegedly stealing  furniture from a vacant house. A scuffle broke out when the officer refused to get an arrest warrant and decided to just take the boy with him.

The officer had the boy by the hand so hard that the child was crying. The mother, Ercilia Zarate, tried to make the officer let go of her son, but Baggett instead started wrestling with Mrs. Zarate. At this moment, Gilbert Zarate, Sr. came in the door from work and saw the officer struggling with his wife and twisting the arm of his son, Gilbert, Jr. Like any father, he went to the defense of his family. The Zarates were later charged with "hindering an officer", even though the boy was never charged with any crime.

# THROUGH BROWN EYES

Chicano politics, being what it is POLITICS, had reached a point where there were cliques of people who were trying to use the fact that they were Chicano to their own personal advantage and to the Chicano people's disadvantage. The Brown Berets chose not to become involved in the infighting among those individuals and organizations in the Chicano community. We decided that political, social, and economic differences among Chicanos were of no consequences to us and our sole motivation and concern would always be the Chicano Movement. We therefore issued the following communique during that period:

"No longer will the Organization involve itself in 'campaigns' against individuals, but the Organization reserves the right to give opinion on any issue.

No longer will the Organization affiliate itself with any other organization for any reason less than an issue that is to the benefit of the Chicano community, or poor/working class community.

The purpose of the Brown berets is to expose and identify problems which plague the Chicano community. And, to offer assistance and/or direction to those Chicanos who suffer due to the insensitivity of the system and the law."

On November 29, 1978, The Dallas Times Herald had an article in it which stated that John L. Hill, Texas Attorney General, released findings in an investigation into the deaths of ten (10) Chicanos or Mexicanos at the hands of Texas officers. The report concluded "that at least three of the deaths were unjustified and that another was probably white washed by a one-sided local investigation."

The deaths of Jesus Martinez Gallegos, Jose Campos Torres, and Ricardo Morales, who was fatally shot by Castroville Police Chief, Frank Haynes in 1975, were the unjustified cases. Larry

# THROUGH BROWN EYES

---

Ortega Lozano's death was the one the Attorney General felt had been white-washed.

On December 08, 1978, Isidro Aguinagas, 40, and his wife Rachel, 27, took their child to the Public Health Clinic in Dimmit, Texas. There Dr. B. D. Murphy diagnosed the baby as seriously ill with respiratory infections and told the parents to take the child across the street immediately to Plains Memorial, the County Hospital.

The family said they pleaded for half an hour with Jack Newsome, administrator of the hospital, to admit the child, promising to pay for the child's care later. Newsome refused. Within hours, the child was dead.

Newsome was later charged with a misdemeanor offense that carries a maximum penalty of a $200 fine.

"This is the same kind of cases where we are dealing with a prevalent attitude in Texas - indifference towards the lives of Mexican-Americans", said Senator Carlos Truan of Corpus Christi, Chairman of the Senate Committee on Rural Health Care.

... Yes, the same kind of attitude: 1978: Juan Benito Martinez, killed, Laredo, Texas... August 01, Paul Martinez, killed, Perryton, Texas... August 22, Jesus Martinez Gallegos, killed Waco, Texas... October 02, Adan Hernandez, killed, Houston, Texas... October l5, Gilbert Zarate, Jr., abused, Cockrell Hill, Texas... November 20, Julio Zamora, Carolyn Valderas, beaten, Dallas, Texas... When will it end????????

# *THROUGH BROWN EYES*

## MY RIGHTS

I SEE MYSELF IN A WORLD THAT'S INDIFFERENT

TO MY THOUGHTS,

       MY IDEAS,

       MY OPINIONS,

          MY CULTURE,

             MY LIFE.

THEY WANT ME TO FOLLOW A SYSTEM
THAT'S GEARED

       TO THEIR LIFE STYLE.

          A    SYSTEM    THAT ALLOWS ME

          ONLY SO FAR

          WITHIN IT.

BUT I TRY TO WORK WITHIN THEIR WORLD,

       THEIR SYSTEM.

I TRY TO SHOW THEM THAT I WANT TO LIVE

             AND
       WORK
       PEACEFULLY.

EVEN IN MY ENDEAVOR TO
FOLLOW THEIR "RULES",

THEIR "SYSTEM", THEIR "LAWS"
THEY RIDICULE ME

AND TELL ME THAT....

.... I'M WRONG

THEY QUESTION MY ENDEAVOR

AND OFFER
ME ALTERNATIVES....

....AND COMPROMISES THAT
LESSEN THE EFFECT

OF MY RESOLUTIONS.

WHAT SHOULD I DO?

SHOULD I ACCEPT THEIR
ALTERNATIVES?

THEIR
COMPROMISES?

KNOWING THAT I WILL ALWAYS
HAVE TO COMPROMISE

OR

SHOULD I MAKE A STAND IN

MY BELIEF,

MY OPINION,

MY CULTURE, AND BY DOING SO,

SHOWING THEM THAT I AM READY
TO FIGHT FOR

MY LIFE!

YES!

I WILL FIGHT!

I AM A MAN!

I AM CHICANO AND MUST BE
LISTENED TO

OR

I WILL

DIE IN

MY EFFORT

TO DO

SO.

BUT THEY WILL NOT WIN!

FOR WHEN I DIE

THERE    WILL
BE OTHERS

TO TAKE MY PLACE.

# THROUGH BROWN EYES

# THROUGH BROWN EYES

# THROUGH BROWN EYES

KESS

Marcos Rodriguez

"Because of KESS's undiminishing efforts to be, not only a part of the Hispanic population of Dallas, but a part that is an asset and an incentive to La Raza, the Organization of the Brown Berets respectfully invite you to attend a cultural event to accept a plague of recognition.

Our invitation is also extended to your news director, Orlando Almanza. His hard work and personality are examples of what it takes to make KESS a true part of La Communidad Chicana. We also have a plaque in his name and invite him to attend said event and receive it."

This was a part of a letter of invitation to Sr. Rodriguez to an event coordinated by the Brown Berets in conjunction with the

REDWIND Community Arts Theatre. The Theatre group held the World Premiere production of "Las Many Muertes of Richard Morales." At this showing the theatre group allowed the Brown Berets to make presentations of plaques to individuals.

Three individuals were selected for reception of seldom given (by the Brown Berets) recognitions. Those who know the Berets understand that the highest honor a Brown Beret can bestow on anyone is to recognize the importance of that individual in La Causa.

Marcos Rodriguez, General Manager of Radio Station KESS, 94FM, was invited to accept the plaque in recognition for his efforts through the radio station. Radio KESS has been instrumental in providing a large volume of information and education to La Raza. KESS has also always been at the disposal of La Raza at times of need. Sr. Rodriguez, in the opinion of the Brown Berets, is the epitome of Radio KESS.

Orlando Almanza, was also selected for his role with KESS. Almanza is a firm believer in giving all parties involved the opportunity on the radio. Also his eagerness to get to the truth in all stories he reports has won him the respect of many, including the Brown Berets.

Joe Landin, Sr. was selected because of his long involvement in the Movement. Sr.

Landin is an example of what all Chicanos could do in the Movement if they wanted to. Endurance and patience are among his many good qualities.

In this book I want to recognize the importance of the REDWIND COMMUNITY ARTS THEATRE, and its director **Eduardo Contreras.**

# THROUGH BROWN EYES

The Redwind Community Arts Theatre is Dallas' only bi-lingual (Spanish-English) theatre. A pamphlet by the group, reads "since its inception, the theatre has entertained enthusiastic audiences with performances at colleges and universities, parks, churches, and other public recreation facilities." The theatre group is exceptional and highly professional, as is the Director Eduardo Contreras.

"I was born in the barrio and while learning classical dance at El Centro (a Junior college in Dallas), I became aware of the tremendous need for something like this for others like me who may never be exposed to it in a formal way," the 31-year-old Dallasite said. "There's a huge potential of talent among our people that never surfaces because nobody will take the time to look for it." As always Contreras' concerns are more about the Theatre and La Raza.

On the 3rd and 4th of February, 1979, the Tejas Brown Berets Organization held a State Conference in Dallas, and Chapters from over thirty cities sent representatives.

February 14, 1979, became another dark day in the course of the Movement. Even though Texas Attorney General, John Hill, ruled that Jesus Martinez Gallegos' death was unjustified and despite U. S. Justice Department pleas for an indictment, a Federal Grand Jury no-billed Waco Policeman, Keith Reed, in the August 22, 1978, killing. There is no justice where respect for the law is ignored.

March was not a good month for Chicanos, but especially not for Pedro Valdez Juarez. Here is his story:

# THROUGH BROWN EYES

Around 8:30 p.m. on March 8, 1979 at 4414 South St. Augustine, the Spruce Square Apts., in Pleasant Grove, Pedro Valdez Juarez noticed a male person at the hood of his car, apparently trying to open it.

Having "been a victim of three cases of stolen batteries and one burglarized apartment", Pedro went into his apartment (41063) to get his 44 magnum pistol. But Pedro changed his mind. "Instead of shooting the person...whom I seen at my car, I just called the police."

Belia, Pedro's sister who was visiting, "had already called my parents to pick me up", heard a knock at the door, and Pedro (who had just come in and called the police) thought it might be the guy he had seen at his car, so he pointed the gun towards the door. Belia "looked through the peep hole and I yelled at my brother and told him that it was only my parents".

"I then went in the restroom to unload my gun", said Pedro. With his parents there was also Rachel Villegas, Pedro's other sister.

Belia then informed her father, Alberto Juarez, that Pedro was "in the bathroom and he has got the gun". She said "I told them that he was mad at some guy who was stealing his battery again".

Armando Villegas arrived at this time and noticed his in-laws were "trying to persuade Pedro to come out of the restroom". "Before I knew it" said Pedro (who was in the bathroom unloading his gun, with the door shut) "my parents had arrived" and "were telling me to come out, that everything was alright".

Before Pedro had finished unloading the gun and preparing it to put it up, there was a knock at the door of the apartment (which Pedro had not heard due to the bathroom door being closed.).

# THROUGH BROWN EYES

Belia went to answer the door when the persons on the outside identified themselves as police. They asked, as they walked into the apartment (apparently no one remembers anybody asking them to come in), if anybody there had called the police about some shots being fired.

Belia then informed them of Pedro's call concerning the battery theft attempt. The police "then told my father to tell Pedro they wanted to talk to him. They asked where he as at. We said in the bathroom. They then told Pedro's father to call him (Pedro) out so they could talk to him."

By this time Pedro had prepared his gun so he could put it up. He heard his father call him and opened the door. He had the gun in his right hand (by the handle, and with the cylinder open). He started to step out of the bathroom when he noticed (standing behind his father) someone in a blue suit ("which I thought was my brother because he usually wears suits like those", said Pedro). Then "I noticed that it was a policeman. I suddenly froze, thinking that he might not understand the gun in my hand, which I was going to take to the closet to put up.

An officer yelled "he's got a gun". They drew their pistols and everybody started screaming and yelling. (The police apparently told Pedro to drop the unloaded gun) but all that he heard in his shocked state was yelling and screaming and crying. He apparently, according to Armando and Rachel Villegas, said he was going to drop the gun. But before he could the second officer, which Pedro could not see, shot him in the hand. The force threw him around and "knocked me back hitting the basin" with his head.

After Pedro regained consciousness, he was ordered to "throw away the other gun". In pain, Pedro cried that there was no "other gun". They ordered him to crawl out, which he did while in pain, bleeding and scared. As he reached the carpet outside the bathroom door, one of the officers jumped on his wounded hand, screaming "try anything and I'll blow your head off".

From the time of the shot, till Pedro regained consciousness, the family was told to leave the apartment, but Pedro's father, who came back to see what was happening to his son, said that "after he was on the stretcher and out of the apartment, I saw the policeman trying to put a shoulder holster on him to get a picture." Of this Pedro remembers "they tried putting on a holster which was hanging outside the restroom on a coat rack right by the door of the restroom. I grabbed both my arms hugging and struggling myself not letting them put it on me."

Pedro also reported being verbally abused by a "Mexican" officer who kept threatening him and saying "we should of just blown your head off".

The officers even harassed him at the hospital, according to Pedro's affidavit, "while surgeon was amputating finger, policeman kept hurrying surgeon". The "surgeon" had to ask the police to leave. After this Pedro heard someone say "we've got to keep him in hospital". He also heard a policeman say "there's no way we're going to leave him here because he tried to kill a policeman". A piece of the bullet is still in his hand at the time of this writing.

After the police realized what they had done, they "covered up" their mistake by charging Pedro with aggravated assault. They also lied to their superiors by saying that Pedro was a "despondent" who "was going to kill himself and take somebody with him."

# THROUGH BROWN EYES

Since when is it a crime for a citizen to carry an unloaded (and with the cylinder open) gun in his own place of residence.

And, since when is it legal for a policeman to walk into any place of residence without permission, or a search warrant, or at least a crime in progress?

If those officers had not entered the Juarez residence without an invitation, they would not have misunderstood Pedro's empty gun, and subsequently shot and arrested him for alleged "aggravated assault" on officers.

The Brown Berets were very instrumental in helping the family file complaints and explaining the law.

The U. S. Justice Department began a renewed search for evidence in the politically sensitive Larry Ortega Lozano case, although Federal officials probing the West Texas jail death of the Mexican-American prisoner had completed their inquiries more than six months before. Strong skepticism of this decision became evident through community reaction. The Berets released a statement calling the "renewed" effort a "farce", date April 11, 1979.

Today, May l6, 1979, we found out through new sources that the two officers found guilty in the Randall Alan Webster's case were sentenced to five years in prison for the killing of the youth from Louisiana, and then the sentence was reduced to probation. Once again, justice prevails?

While all this was going on, two Fort Worth police officers were systematically stealing money from undocumented workers at a South Fort Worth Motel known as a haven for prostitutes.

The officers would wait for an undocumented worker to take a prostitute into a room at the motel, located in the M00 block of East Rosdale, then would burst into the room and demand identification.

# THROUGH BROWN EYES

When the worker handed over his wallet, the officers would remove any cash, give it back and leave the room. They (the police) were suspended and charged with official misconduct.

This case provided us with something to playfully make fun of police. But in any case, we still did not overlook the reinforcement that there were, are, and will be officers who will misuse their authority and obligation.

### *!! KILLER SET FREE!!*

September 12, 1979

Darrell L. Cain, Ex-Dallas Police Officer, who in July 1973 shot and killed Santos Rodriquez, a 12-year-old Chicano, was discharged Tuesday from the Department of Corrections facility in Huntsville. He served only 272 years for the murder. There is no Justice!!

It was on October 5, 1979, a Federal appeals Court ordered U. S. District Judge Ross N. Sterling to imprison three former Houston Officers whose sentences he suspended after they were convicted in the drowning of Jose Campos Torres. But, it was on October 30, 1979, that Sterling made a "mockery of justice" by sentencing the killers of the 21-year-old Chicano to one year and one day. Justice, or Just Us??

1979 found us involved in many local cases. From helping file complaints against the police to translating to distributing educational materials to La Raza. Also during this year the Brown Berets throughout the State had been attending "Police-Community" symposiums organized by the Justice Department's Community Relations Service.

In November, 1979, the Brown Berets from Dallas, Lubbock, Fort Worth, Austin, and Big Spring attended a symposium in Fort

Worth. The members attended the function with full intention of remaining throughout the gatherings. But on the second day, the symposium organizers had Assistant Attorney Drew Days III as speaker.

A little after Days speech started the Berets and supporters, over 20 persons, walked out on his speech. "We're not going to listen to this man. It's people such as Drew Days that have been directly involved in creating the problems we have today."

Drew Days was primarily responsible for the Justice Department dropping the Santos Rodriguez case. We even agreed with Houston Police Chief Harry Caldwell who said "I have no confidence whatsoever in the United States government or the Justice Department to handle this on a national level."

Locally, the Berets were also having meetings with the police. During the symposium mentioned above, then Capt. Jack Revil of the Internal Affairs Department, gave a speech in which he seemed to call for the community to get involved in improving relations between the community and the police. The agreements reached between us and the police gave us some hope for at least local improvement.

"We really wanted", we said "A Citizen's Review Board, which we believe is the only answer, but seems to be an unobtainable goal at this moment. So, instead, we've compromised and maintained the lines of communication open between us."

"So many," we added "of our people in need of police assistance can speak better in Spanish than in English and find all the forms they have to fill out in filing complaints too confusing. These people become discouraged in filing and receive no help in filling out the forms. They give up and go home." On this, the Internal Affairs Division informed us that they would henceforth accept affidavits in Spanish. They also transferred a Chicano to the I.A.D. to assist Spanish speakers. The Officer is Joe Rodriguez.

"Another thing," we continued "those needing to file a complaint with the Internal Affairs Division had to go downtown to the main police station. This practice forces the complainant to miss work (in many cases), also, persons have to pay for parking or transportation, causing further burden on those who are already economically deprived."

Capt. Revil said that department policy allows any police supervisor in any office, including the sub-districts, to accept complaints. And, he added, because there are supervisors on duty at all times, citizens can file complaints 24 hours a day.

"The rule", we agreed "has been a rule for years that has never been enforced, and we simply asked them to comply with it. They agreed to it." Will wonders never cease?

One of the bigger events in 1979, besides the takeover of the "Nest of Spies," was the March for Human Dignity in Dallas.

I believe it was in late September that I was called by Victor Bonilla. He told me that he had received word that the Klan was attempting to get permission to march in Dallas. My first reaction was to call Bill Stoner and Charlie Young. Young told me that if we were going to be planning something in conjunction with the Klan

March to count the Patriots in. Bill's response was to recommend that we hold a meeting at Martin Luther King Center, in South Dallas, to consider any action.

At the meeting we came to a few conclusions: First, we assigned someone to find out for sure if the Klan had really applied for a parade permit and whether or not they would receive approval. Secondly, just in case they would receive approval we assigned others to consider a route to be proposed to us at our next meeting.

Finally, depending on the approval or disapproval of the Klan permit, we assigned others to make initial, tentative contacts for support from the groups and individuals.

Once we were sure that the Klan permit was approved, everything started to fall in place. We had meetings all throughout October. The meetings were well structured, well planned, and well implemented.

From seven persons at the first meeting the list of supporters and endorsers grew.

The final list included the following: Texas Farmworkers Union; Fredrick Douglas Voting Council; Black Women's United Front; Texas Tenant's Union; I.M.A.G.E.; S.C.E.F.; Progressive Voters League; Tejas Brown Berets Organization; Bois d'Arc Patriots; N.A.A.C.P.; American G.I. Forum; Tarrant County Tenant's Union; Skip Johnson of the United League of Mississippi; Houston Prisoners Solidarity Committee; Austin Prisoners Solidarity Committee; National Fight Back; Prisoners United for Justice for Prisoners; Gay Political Caucus; L.U.L.A.C. 4272; L.U.L.A.C. of Garland; Clergy and Laity Concerned; Jewish Student Association of S.M.U.; Committee of Justice; State Rep., Lanell Cofer; State Rep., Paul Ragsdale; D.C.C.A. Director Arron Floyd; Bill Stoner, UHURU Family; Reverend Zan Holmes; American Indian Center's, Mike Methetsky; East Dallas Tenants Union; American Liberation

Seminar; Mexican-American Assembly for Civil Involvement; U. S. Congressman, Micky Leland, Hornets Motorcycle Club; Chicano Voters League. El Pueblo Newspaper in San Antonio; Buffalo Soldiers Motorcycle Club; National People's Alliance, Raza Unida-Dallas; Raza Unida-State; Labor Council for Latin American Advancement; Robert Medrano; Fuerza de Dallas; Centro de Accion; Mexican-American Student Organization of El Centro College; Hispanic Business and Professional Committee for Justice; A.F.S.M.E. - Dallas; Students of Holy Trinity Seminar; Council Woman, Elsie Faye Heggins; Reverend Mark Herbener; Better Influence Association of Fort Worth; Center for Constitutional Rights; Reverend A. H. Forbes; Dr. Eddie C. G. Davis, D.P.M.; N.O.W. Board member, Barbara Eckberg; Georgia State Senator, Julian Bond; St. John's Baptist Church's, Dr. Robert Wilson; S.C.L.C. Pres., Dr. Joseph Lowry; Southwest Oak Cliff Development Center; and the East Texas Chapter of the National Lawyers Guild.

It was no wonder that we had up to 3,000 persons attending the Anti-Klan March.

A light point in this story happened just before we started our March. I was listening to the walkie-talkies for information on the Klan's March. They started from the Old City Hall on Harwood, and we were behind the new City Hall. I received a message that the Klan March had 800 people. We could see the helicopters overhead. I started getting worried. I didn't know that the Klan had that much support in Dallas.

"Hold that last message," came the voice on the walkie-talkie" those 800 people...they're not marching with the Klan, they're chasing them!!" We found out later that the police had to take the Klan under the County Building because those chasing them were beginning to seem violent.

# THROUGH BROWN EYES

"List of the Victims" continues: March 08, 1979, Pedro Valdez Juarez, shot, Dallas, Texas...March 18, Benito Rincon, Efren Reyes, killed, Mexican Border, Texas... April 22, Danny Elliot, killed, Dallas, Texas... May 23, Jack Marvin, beaten, Dallas, Texas... May 27, Joe Rodriguez, killed, Denver, Colorado... June 29, Juan and Belia Iruegas, beaten, Dallas, Texas... July 24, Reynaldo Rodriguez, James Gomez, Mary Jessie Cipriano, and Audelai Cipriano, abused, Dallas, Texas... August 1, Gril Couch, killed, Austin, Texas... August, Vicente Trujillo, killed, Austin, Texas... August 18, Marco Montoya and Eladio Herrera, beaten, Jackie Rosales and Eustorgio Montoya, abused, Dallas, Texas...

## BUT WHEN I DIE

There Are Many Things To Accomplish

In Life. I Have Accomplished Only

A Few Of The Many Things I Want To Do.


I Want To Live To See The Day When

My People Can Be Men And Women

Able To Choose And Live As They Want.


I Want To Live To See The Day When

All Bigotry, Discrimination, Prejudice,

And Racist Intentions Are Abolished.


I Want To Live To See The Day When

The Hungry Are Fed, When The Sick

Are Cured, When We All Can Be Humans.


Some Day I Must Die, For Whatever

Reason Destiny Dictates. I Want To

Die Satisfied I've Accomplished For La Raza.

# THROUGH BROWN EYES

---

But When I Die, My Goals Will Not Die,

For Somewhere Some Child Will Be Born

And He Will Also Follow These Goals.


He Will Not Be Stopped. For Even If

He Dies Others Will Follow. If I Must

Die, So Be It, As Long As La Raza Lives.

LA ONDA

Dallas Bown Berets

NO. 14

CHICANA

GRATIS - FREE

LAS

Brown

Berets

## *Chapter 12*

## *THE YEAR OF THE MONKEY, Part I*

The beginning of this year was quite a bit out of the ordinary, mainly because of the Iranian situation.

Because of the hysteria, which was prevalent during this period, over the hostages, and over the Shah being in San Antonio, the Organization decided to issue the following communique:

"IRAN: THE DEPOSED SHAH"

"The Brown Berets Organization feels that by maintaining the Shah in the U.S., the government is showing us that they care less about us, as well as those detained in Iran."

"His being here is an INSULT to all citizens, especially to Chicano, Black and poor peoples. The U. S. worries about the Shah's human rights, but has continually deprived many U. S. citizens of their rights. The Shah is a criminal who should be returned to Iran. Nobody wants him here."

"Many Black Activists support this position, they also have seen the racism that has manifested itself in the people involved in this case."

"With strong determination we call upon the U. S. government to send the Shah back to Iran, and maintain dignity within our own peoples."

The Tejas Brown Berets also stated that they fully understood the reasons for the Embassy take over. They also declared themselves in solidarity with the Iranian Revolution against imperialism, and all Third World Movements.

The unusualness started while we were in Austin at a Brown Beret Conference. Charlie Young, of the Bois d'Arc Patriots, called and let me know that there was a group who was planning to go to Iran. He also said that he had told them that I might be interested in going, too.

After I had gotten phone numbers and other necessary information from Charlie, I got in contact with Rusty Davenport, who was helping making arrangements for those who had been invited to go to Iran. He told me that I had to be in New York by the next day, February 05, 1980.

After the conference, we went home and my wife, Lydia, and I got my things ready for the trip. It turned out that I had to catch a plane at almost 3:00 in the morning.

I arrived in New York City very early. Even as the plane was coming in for a landing, I was struck with the enormity of the City. Up until now, I had been used to calling Houston, and Dallas big cities, but, from now on, they will always be medium sized cities to me.

I arrived at agreed address in downtown, Manhattan. I went up to the U. S. Passport Office, and had my passport within forty minutes. There were men who we believed were State Department people helping us process the passports quickly.

It seemed that I had gotten prepared to leave a day earlier. Many others who were planning to go, were still arriving, and would continue to arrive until the next day.

# THROUGH BROWN EYES

Rick Diehl, with the Mountain Community Union of Morgantown, West Virginia, was extremely helpful to me. First of all, he told me that I wouldn't have to worry about where I could stay

the night. He said I could stay at an apartment that was lent to him. He also gave me a sort of tour of New York. He had some business around town and I stuck to him. Seeing the City first hand, I had that feeling of awesomeness and enormity. But, as Rick put it to me, "just act normal".

The next day we were gathered at our meeting place. We were informed of certain things we were to know, such as how to act with Iranians, some of their customs, and such.

We left that evening on our trip.

After my return, I stayed quite busy between my duties as Public Relations Coordinator and my obligation to share with the public what I learned in Iran.

# THROUGH BROWN EYES

Ernesto "Che" Guevara, once said, in a letter to his children, "above all, always abhor any injustice committed against anyone, anywhere in the world." I totally believe in that philosophy, so hence my obligation to do something about it.

From February 18, 1980 to April 25, 1980, I made almost twenty presentations on my trip to Tehran. Also, during these presentations, I was frequently asked about the Brown Berets, thereby providing me with ample opportunity to talk about the Organization and La Causa.

If nothing else, I was able to learn the truth of what was happening. Now I know that the Brown Berets and the Chicano Movement are correct in their struggle against Imperialism, the cancer of the world.

The Iranian issue did not, though, effect the momentum of the movement. For example, Chicano Activist, Carlos Montes, who was accused of allegedly being involved in a fire at the Biltmore Hotel in Los Angeles, where the then Governor, Ronald Reagan, was speaking, was declared innocent of all charges. Montes' lawyers said that evidence showed that the fire was provoked by Agent Fernando Sumaya, who infiltrated the Brown Berets with intention of discrediting the Organization.

The San Antonio Brown Berets were keeping very busy with an issue which effects all people in all cities, crime. An article titled "Rooting out trouble in the barrio" by Mike Greenberg, in the The News, a San Antonio newspaper, describes a situation in which youth gangs are becomming a serious problem to parts of San Antonio. Different people, including the police offered a variety of solutions, including coming down hard on the "offenders" and even sending them off to jail or prison. The Brown Berets, the paper says, "put the heat on everybody to help the troublemakers rather than exile them."

"The Brown Berets got involved in San Juan a few weeks ago," said the news article, "No longer the militant anti-establishment organization it was 10 years ago, the Brown Berets have only about

# THROUGH BROWN EYES

20 members in San Antonio. Its leaders are articulate, intelligent men in their 20's and 30's. Remnants of the old militant ideology hang on in their speech.

"These people are not being listened to," Beret member Adolph de la Santos says. Families are being asked to leave. These kids are rebelling against the system. There is no way out for them. When they set fire to the trash in a dumpster, the authorities say it's because they're looking for trouble, or because their mothers are lazy. It's because the dumpsters are full and trash is piling up on the ground."

"The Brown Berets say they want to work with kids, find out what's bothering them, present positive images.

"The Brown Berets criticize the city for closing the recreation center and counseling offices at 5 p.m. "That's when these guys come out," de la Santos says. They say the policy of excluding troublemakers from the recreation center in effect abandons the kids who need help the most."

Another article from The News, in San Antonio, dated March 05, 1980, titled "Brown Beret Says: WE WILL FIGHT KID GANGSTERS", and written by Jim Martin, News Staff Writer, gives yet another view on this same matter:

"A 'soldier' in a West Side para-military group has pledged his organization to a bare-knuckle battle in war against youth-gang violence.

"Suggestions of a curfew to corral the gangs "would start the kids shooting at police instead of each other," the Brown Beret warns.

# THROUGH BROWN EYES

"Victor San Miguel, who described himself as a "soldier" in the barrio organization, told San Juan Homes residents the Brown Berets are willing to work with youths in the housing project.

"About 75 San Juan residents met with city officials Tuesday to discuss ways to deal with marauding youths who have forced at least a dozen families to leave the neighborhood.

"Several residents told City Councilman Bernardo Eureste and San Antonio Housing Authority Director Apolino Flores they want curfew.

"Eureste said city and SAHA lawyers would meet to discuss the legality of a curfew.

"CURFEW

"If they have a curfew, there will be more cops in here," San Miguel told The News.

"The kids don't know how to deal with the cops. They just say, 'We're going to get guns and shoot back.' When police go into the courts now, the kids throw rocks at them."

"San Miguel said his group would be more successful than the police in finding out who the young toughs are and straightening them out.

"If they want to fight, we'll get it on with them barehanded," San Miguel said.

"The police over here use Gestapo tactics," said one San Juan resident who asked not to be identified.

"People won't cooperate with the cops because the cops harass them. They never get here in time to catch the one who does the shooting or the stabbing. They just arrest everyone nearby (the crime scene)," the resident said.

"Some of the younger people at the meeting claimed there are no organized gangs and the problem has been blown out of proportion.

"Nobody can tell me there isn't a problem," an agitated Eureste snapped.

"'I was driving through this neighborhood about 10:30 at night when I was pulled over and asked to break up a shootout.

"'I've talked to families who fear for their lives," the councilman said.

"'I guarantee you can expect to be shot in the back by someone you don't even know while walking down Zarzamora or Brady streets.

"Eureste said he didn't have a ready solution but told the group he was "committed to finding one.

"The councilman said he welcomed the help of the Brown Berets 'or anybody else who will work with us and help.

On April 03, 1980, Hijinio Veloz, l7, allegedly shot and killed 45-year-old Decatur Policeman, James Leroy Bennett. The family called the Berets for whatever assistance was possible. They did not want him sentenced to death, if possible.

An article in the Fort Worth Star Telegram, titled "'Fair Trial' concern for Brown Berets", gave a report on action taken by the Brown Berets.

# *THROUGH BROWN EYES*

"Decatur - The Dallas chapter of the Brown Berets, a politically active Mexican-American group, has sent letters to officials expressing concern for a fair trial for Hijinio Veloz Jr., who is accused of the capital murder of a Decatur police officer. Brown Beret spokesman Juan Perez of Dallas said the letters asked that "equal justice" be applied to Veloz's case, "the same justice that was applied to Darrell Cain."

"Perez referred to Dallas police officer Darrell Cain, who was convicted of shooting to death a 12-year-old boy in July 1973 as the youth sat handcuffed in the rear seat of a squad car (actually, readers, Santos was in the front seat of the car -JMP). The Brown Berets protested as too light the five-year sentence assessed Cain by a State Court Jury."

"We're not attacking the police as far as the law is concerned," Perez said. "But since we are supposed to be living in a system in which justice allegedly applies to all persons equally, we just want to make sure that justice is applied to Hijinio Veloz as well." Veloz, 17, remains in Wise County jail without bond on a capital murder indictment charging him with the April 3 slaying of Decatur patrolman James Leroy Bennett, 45.

"Veloz pleaded not guilty during a Monday arraignment. His attorney, Jim Sawyer of Fort Worth, said he will try to move the trial to another city.

"We believe that laws should apply equally to all citizens," said Perez. "And that means that an officer should be no more equal than a citizen. A capital murder charge makes the officer more equal."

"Decatur officials offered no comment on the Brown Beret letters. Police Chief James Fellers said District Attorney Smith had advised all involved in the case "not to talk about it until after the trial was over."

The "letters" that are referred to in the article were in actuality leaflets that were sent to the city officials and other interested entities of the City of Decatur. I have included the leaflet in its entirety:

"JUSTICE"

"Once again we are going to see the injustice of this system in action.

"17-year-old Hijinio Veloz allegedly shot and killed 45-year-old James Bennett in Decatur. Bennett was a police officer. Will there be justice?

"A Dallas Police Officer was found guilty and convicted of murdering a handcuffed twelve-year-old boy. Santos Rodriguez was already in the front seat of squad car when Cain placed a .357

magnum to the boy's head and "blew his brains out." Was there justice?

"Darryl Cain was sentenced to 5-years and served only two-and-a-half (2 ½) years. Justice?

"We predict that Hijinio Veloz will not receive a fair trial by his peers.

"We predict that Hijinio Veloz will be tried by an all-White or majority White, Jury!

"We predict that racism, and not justice, will be the basis of this sentencing.

"We challenge the system to prove us wrong! We dare say you won't!

"We call upon all people to demand equally enforced, equally applied laws.

"There is no police officer that is better than, more important than, or more equal than the youngest Chicano child.

"VIVA LA JUSTICIA!

"VIVA AZTLAN LIBRE!

"DALLAS BROWN BERETS 337-4135" *(This number is now out of order)*

Hijinio Veloz was found guilty by an all-White jury and sentenced to life imprisonment. If you kill a cop, you get life imprisonment or the death sentence, but if a cop kills you he may serve 2½ years at the most. Racism and discrimination, 100%.

Well, on April 26, the police announced, they would be holding a "Police-Hispanic" Conference. I received a letter from Police Capt.

C. S. Bridges inviting me to the gathering. His letter and our response are included here:

"April 11, 1980

"Dear Mr. Perez:

"You are invited to attend a conference sponsored by the Dallas Police Department in an effort to bring police officials and Hispanic community members together to examine mutual concerns and to explore constructive relationships.

"The meeting will take place on Saturday, April 26, 1980 from 9:00 a.m. to 5:00 p.m., at the Dunfey Dallas Hotel, 3800 West Northwest Highway, Dallas, Texas.

"The first step in overcoming negative images, distrust and alienation is to take an honest look at the issues that have tended to divide us. The enclosed tentative program draft sets forth three topics selected for discussion at this meeting.

"Formal presentations will be made on each of the selected subjects by law enforcement officials, portion of our time has been set aside for dialogue and presentation of recommendations by the participants.

"If there are other topics of discussion of interest to participants they can hopefully be discussed at future meetings of this type.

"There is no intention at this conference to discuss details of specific police-citizen incidents. There will be no debate regarding the guilt or innocence of any parties alleged to have committed wrongful acts. We want honest dialogue and objective evaluation on the issues.

"Enclosed is a copy of the program agenda for your information. We also request that you complete the enclosed card, indicating if you will attend the conference, and return it to us as soon as possible in the enclosed envelope. Lunch will be provided for you at the conference site and we need to make reservations for participants in advance.

"I sincerely hope that you will be able to participate in this conference. If you have any questions or need further clarification on the conference, don't hesitate to contact conference coordinator, Captain C. S. Bridges, Police Community Services Division, 670-4427.

The Brown Berets response was:

"Dear Sir,

"I have been requested by the Brown Berets Organization to obtain more information on the upcoming conference.

"We are unclear as to the objective(s) of the conference. For example: These recommendations, who will they be made to, what will be done about them, and who will make the decisions on them.

"Also, the structure of your agenda is very similar to the one used by the Justice Department's "Police/Community Conference" agenda. Their conferences were a waste of tax money, with nothing more achieved than "dialogue", unfulfilled "recommendations", and "objective evaluations". We would have liked to have come up with something much more substantial.

"As far as the "Selection Process for Police Recruits" is concerned, it makes no difference what color, race or sex the officer is, as long as the law is enforced equally for all citizens, without discrimination of any sort.

"Likewise, "Selection and Training Methods" are unimportant in comparison to the law being applied equally to all citizens. Neither of these subjects is actually a solution to the problem of police abuse of citizens, especially the non-major race and poor citizens.

"An officer's personal opinions should be his, and not the public's concern, though we, of course, would prefer mature, responsible persons as police. An officer's actions, on the other hand, should be everyone's concern.

"As far as "Force, It's Use and Control", this is the issue, and to the best of our knowledge there are only 3 realistic solutions:

"1) Develop and establish a policy that would restrict an officer from using excessive or deadly force on anyone, except in the case(s) where a life is in obvious, provable danger.

"2) The creation of a "Uniform Sentencing" law, where all persons (regardless of race, color, sex, occupation, or economic status) who commit the same crime would receive the sentence.

"The way that both the community groups and the police in Dallas can play a realistic role in this effort, is for both groups to announce publicly their support for the "Uniform Sentencing Law", and their commitment to work for its implementation.

"3) The creation of a workable, community elected, Citizen's Review Board. It could investigate all complaints against the police by citizens.

"If the Dallas Police Department is ready to "dialogue" on realistic solutions to police brutality, then we are too.

"Your letter doesn't suggest any solution, so we've offered three.

"Can you assure us that the police will consider our proposals? At all the Justice Department's conferences the police officials, the sheriffs and chiefs, showed their unwillingness to consider actually working for any of these solutions. We on the other hand, have considered and found holes in their alleged solutions.

"Finally, if we can be assured of the above, we would be happy to arrive at 12:30 to your conference and stay to the end of your workshop on "Force, It's Use and Control".

"As this is a public matter we are providing the news media with any and all transactions between yourselves and us on this subject.

"Also, please accept this letter as an official request by the Brown Beret Organization on the following information:

"1) Whose monies are being used to implement this conference?

"2) Which Chicano groups were involved in organizing the conference?

"3) Why are Blacks and working class Whites being excluded? They suffer police brutality too.

"Please answer in writing for our records.

# THROUGH BROWN EYES

"After our response of the 14th of April, Capt. Bridges sent me a letter saying that the invitation was for me, and not the Organization. We responded that "no member of this Organization will ever take individual action on any issue which involves the Brown Berets or La Raza without prior approval and sanction.

Additionally, all invitations of this kind must be sent to the Organization so that the Brown Berets can decide which member is to attend the function.

"In any case, the police refused to assure us that they would make an effort to deal with the subjects that we wanted to talk about. They only wanted to discuss what they thought was important.

"In April, the Dallas Internal Affairs Department started an investigation on recent police shootings. The steady rise in police shootings of citizens is a matter of official concern and has prompted an extensive investigation into police-citizen confrontations, said Capt. William Newman of the I.A.D. "We don't know if it is just our problem, or a nationwide problem. We have been looking, for instance, at Los Angeles, where they are experiencing the same kind of rise."

Bill Stoner, Black Activist, said "Blacks are taking the brunt of all their conference. We're beginning to wonder if there is an 'Open Season' or something going on."

**_Ten_** persons had been shot by Dallas police in only 4 months this year. The persons include January 01, Benny Juan Martinez, 28. He "made a furtive gesture toward his pocket" police alleged. Martinez was shot in the leg. No weapon was found. January 06, Jose Vargas was shot and killed after he was doing some shooting at a park himself. R. D. Thomas, a 24-year-old Black, was shot and killed on January 30. Robert Rollins, a 28-year-old, was already under arrest when a police officer who was holding a gun to Rollins head, said Rollins moved in a threatening gesture so the officer shot him on the head, on February 21. Clifton Mabry, a 21 year-old Black, was shot on March 05, for allegedly pulling a screwdriver on police. On March 05, Paul Wing, also Black, was shot as he slammed a door in the cops face. He was not armed. Richard Taylor, a White 2l-year-old, was shot by officers on the 26th of March. A Black school teacher was shot by police four times, on March 28, killing him. 42-year-old, Ernest Caro, a Black was shot and killed on April 18. Clifford Ray Martin was allegedly beating a woman when police told him to drop a gun he was holding. Police shot and killed the Black 23-year-old, on April 2l.

On April 26, 1980, the Dallas Police Department held its "Police Hispanic" meeting, but not the way they expected it. As the Dallas Morning News said, in an article dated, 04-27-80, "Of the 37 Hispanics King invited, 22 sent letters of acceptance. But in the end, after the Berets spent much of Friday urging those invited not to participate, fewer than 10 Mexican-Americans attended. The group also criticized the location of the conference in an affluent section of North Dallas miles away from the Mexican-American barrio- and said Blacks and Whites were excluded from the invitation list.

The Bois d'Arc Patriots also participated in the picket of the "meeting", along with Black Activist, Bill Stoner, who said that another police conference planned for later in the spring for Blacks also would be boycotted.

# THROUGH BROWN EYES

On May l7, four ex-policeman were acquitted, by an all-White, six-man, jury, in the killing of Black insurance man, Arthur McDuffie. Once again, true ('??) Justice.

This date was also the first day of a "Regional Rebellion" in Miami. The disturbance lasted three days.

All through the killings and the Regional Rebellion, the Brown Berets and the Coalition for a Citizens Review Board were trying to get a Review Board implemented.

Even Dallas Police Chief, Glen D. King, got into the act. He proposed a Citizen Panel empowered to review the work product of Internal Investigations into each allegation of police brutality or unauthorized use of force.

The support for a Citizen's Review Board kept growing. A partial list of groups endorsing the board included: N.A.A.C.P., Mexican-American Assembly for Civic Involvement, Block Partnership, Bois d'Arc Patriots, Brown Berets, Progressive Voters League, La Raza Unida, League of United Latin American Citizens, American Civil Liberties Union, Coalition for Human Dignity and Interdenominational Ministerial Alliance.

"The President of the Dallas Police Association said this week he is against minority group proposals for a Citizen's Review Board to investigate allegations of police violence, but that he might be willing to support a more modest proposal made by Chief Glen King", said an article by the Dallas Times Herald, 06-08-80. "The battleground itself," continued the article later on "is emotional".

In the more than 123 separate police shooting incidents since the killing of Santos Rodriguez, which brought Dallas as near to a race riot as it has been, not one officer has been punished, or even reprimanded.

# THROUGH BROWN EYES

Mansfield, Ohio, June 08, 1980, the N.A.A.C.P. has proposed the creation of a Citizen's Review Board. It seems that an investigative series by the Mansfield News Journal described numerous incidents of police misconduct. Also, the F. B. I. is investigating allegations of police brutality in the city of 56,000 persons.

On June 14, 1980, the Coalition for a Citizen's Review Board held a demonstration at City Hall. The Brown Berets, along with others, provided the security.

The Dallas Police Association voted unanimously to reject the creation of a Civilian Review Board, on June 19, 1980.

1980 was a year that will remain clear in the minds of proponents of Citizen Police Review Boards. On April 2'4, '80, Donald Ray Rogers, 23, was shot and killed by a Dallas Police Officer, making him the 11th killing by police this year in only four (4) months.

Something the reader should understand at this point, is that since the Rogers killing, it was three (3) months before the police shot another citizen in Dallas. This was the same period that the community was calling for a Citizen's Review Board. As soon as the Council voted down the proposal on June 25, '80, the shootings and killings continued in Dallas with the Killing of 18 year-old, Samuel S. Stone on July 15, and, in Euless, with the shooting of 15-year-old David Medellin.

On June 25, 1980, two significant actions occurred. First of all, the Dallas City Council voted down the proposal for a Citizen's Review Board. The vote, as in most cases like this, was along racial lines, 8 Whites voted NO, 2 Blacks and 1 Chicano voted YES. Instead the Council, in an attempt to confuse the public, created a "Police Advisory Committee". The Committee will review investigations by the Police Department's Internal Affairs Division in cases involving death or serious injury.

The second event, one with more serious results, was not only coincidental, but it seemed to emphasis the very reason a Citizen's Review Board is necessary.

On June 26, the day after the Dallas City Council voted down a proposed Citizens Police Review Board, a news release by the Euless Police Department, submitted by Police Chief J. M. Wilson, was made public, describing the police's allegations on a shooting which occurred in Euless.

"On June 25, 1980, at 8:27 P.M., two (2) patrol elements and a sergeant were dispatched on a domestic disturbance call with a knife, at 1374 Raider Drive, Apt. 278. The elements and sergeant arrived at the location at 8:31 P.M.

"They were met in the parking lot by Mr. Felimon Duque, L/M/20, one of the occupants of Apt. 278. He stated that there had been a family fight involving a knife. He had blood on his hands and shirt, but was not injured. He had asked another resident to call the police.

"Sgt. H. C. Westmoreland, Officer T. D. Cottle and Officer S. T. Cantrell then went to Apt. 278. Sgt. Westmoreland knocked and the door was opened by Mr. Rosendo Medellin, L/M/35. The officers observed blood on Mr. Medellin and the apartment was in disarray. They then entered the apartment. Sgt. Westmoreland then asked what the problem was, and for him to produce the knife, if one was involved.

"At that point, David Medellin, L/M/15, who was sitting at a table, reached behind a refrigerator and produced a butcher knife. He then jumped up and began screaming, "I'm going to kill you." The officers told the subject several times to drop the knife.

"The subject then made an attempt to throw the knife at Officer Cantrell. Sgt. Westmoreland and Officer Cottle fired their revolvers almost simultaneously. The subject was struck five times.

"The subject was taken to HEB Hospital by Mid-Cities Ambulance. The case will be taken before the Tarrant County Grand Jury.

"06-26-80, 8:00 A.M.

"Euless Police Department

"J. M. Wilson, Police Chief

This case turned out to be one of those in which everyone involved disagreed with the police's allegations of what actually occurred. In the above report, the police say that David "made an attempt to throw the knife at Officer Cantrell", but statements given to the press at different times, and by different officers, allege that Medellin threw the knife and that it "hit Cantrell, but did not injure him."

Cottle and Westmoreland responded by firing at the youth six times, hitting him with five of the shots. Medellin was wounded twice in the right forearm, once in the left forearm, once in the left pelvis and once in the right thigh.

In an article by C. C. Risenhoover, of the Fort Worth Star Telegram, July 16, 1980, David Medellin told the reporter that "All I know is that the police shot me," he said. "Me and my brother had been in a fight and he went outside. My dad was talking to me, and it sounded like someone was trying to break in the door.

"I remember Dad going to the door and hearing him say that he had everything under control. They (the police) pushed my father away from the door and came in.

"I think I had taken one step to put a knife in the kitchen when I heard shots and felt pain. There were more shots when I was on the floor. I remember hearing my brother say, 'Don't go on us, don't go on us.' Then I vaguely remember the ambulance and the emergency room."

In an article dated June 06, 1980, also from the Fort Worth Star Telegram, and also by C. C. Risenhoover, the reporter interviewed David's 20-year-old, half-brother, Felimon Duque. He also had a different account of what happened.

"My brother and I had an argument and fist fight," said Duque, a carpenter for Dallas Acoustics. "A lady in one of the downstairs apartments called the police department (the police report said that the police "were dispatched on a domestic disturbance call with a knife." Now how did anyone not in the apartment during the fight know that a knife was or was not involved? - J MP)

"Duque said he stopped the police in the parking lot and told them that the trouble had been resolved, that it was just a fight between him and his 15-year-old brother.

"Duque said the police asked him if there were any guns in the house, and he told them, 'No.'

"Duque said the officers went up the stairs and started pounding on the door, but that his father initially refused to open it.

"'He finally opened the door after they had almost broken it down,' Duque said, and told them there was no trouble, that he had taken care of the trouble. They just pushed him out of the way and went into the apartment."

In another part of the article, David's father, Rosendo Medellin, said he tried to stop the police from entering his apartment. "I told them I didn't want them there, but they force their way in," he said. "They busted the door knob."

Both David's father and half-brother, agree that David had a knife in his hand, but "He just picked up a knife and started taking it to the kitchen," said Duque, "and the officers started hollering and shooting at the same time. He did not throw the knife. It fell to the floor when the first bullet struck him."

But, even if what the police claimed in their different reports and statements to reporters is true, and David had thrown a knife at officers, the police themselves admitted that the alleged knife did not injure anyone. So why did they still shoot David six times, hitting him with five bullets?

Another article by C. C. Risenhoover in the Fort Worth Star Telegram details actions that were taken by some individuals and groups in the Chicano community of the Metroplex area. "EULESS - Representatives from three Mexican-American organizations say they want to hear from police here why officers shot a 15-year-old youth five times after a family disturbance.

"The groups will meet Thursday with Euless Police Chief Johnnie Wilson to discuss the June 25 shooting of David Medellin, who is in H-E-B Hospital recovering from five gunshot wounds.

"Police said Medellin was shot after throwing a butcher knife that hit Officer S.T. Cantrell. The officers who fired at the youth were Sgt. H.C. Westmoreland and T.D. Cottle, police said.

"The three police officers had responded to a domestic disturbance call from a downstairs neighbor of Medellin's parents, Rosendo and Josie Medellin.

# THROUGH BROWN EYES

"Juan Perez, spokesman for the Dallas chapter of the Brown Berets, said he and representatives of LULAC and the G.I. Forum will meet with Wilson.

"'There are no particular objectives relating to this meeting,' Perez said. 'We want to hear the police side of the story, to find out why it was necessary to shoot the boy five times.'

"'We're also a little concerned about the internal investigation conducted by Euless police; why the officers were cleared the day after the shooting.'

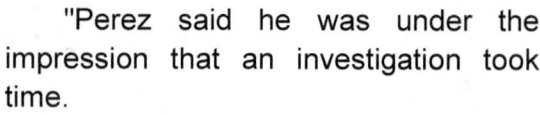

"Perez said he was under the impression that an investigation took time.

"'I also understand,' the Brown Beret spokesman said, 'that a new grand jury is being seated in Tarrant County. If its like grand juries seated in Dallas County, we're concerned that the persons picked won't really have an understanding of both sides of a question.'

"'In Dallas they pick bankers, lawyers, white-collar persons who just don't have much understanding of what is really going on'

"Perez said he was concerned that the grand jury might not let members of the Medellin family testify.

"'The same night David was shot,' Perez said, 'the police had Rosendo to sign an affidavit about what happened. The man doesn't speak English all that well, and he really has trouble reading it.'

# THROUGH BROWN EYES

"'But Rosendo and Felimon (Duque, David's half-brother) say the police account of the shooting is not true,' said Perez.

"The father and the half-brother (who, the police said in the mentioned meeting, were witnesses that support the officers' story - JMP) said Medellin did not throw the knife, that the youth was returning it to the kitchen when the first bullet hit him and knocked it from his hand."

The officers involved in the shooting were no-billed by the Tarrant County Grand Jury. I guess it's all right to shoot unarmed youngsters if you happen to be a police officer, and the youths happen to be Chicano! On June 27, 1980, the Coalition for a Citizen's Review Board decided to put the issue before the City of Dallas for referendum.

The Brown Berets, as well as other groups, decided not to participate actively in the effort, though they wholeheartedly endorsed the effort by the Coalition. When asked our (the Berets) feelings on the decision by the Council, I responded "We're angry and frustrated. There is no other recourse but for the public, in any way necessary, to show the City Council how it feels."

August 11, Clinton Whiteman, 24, shot; August 27, Bobby Williams, shot; September 09, Patricia Henry, killed; October 10, Esteban Valderas, 2l, killed; October 23, Harvey Lee Whitefeild, 16, shot; October 29, Steven Michael Carrel, shot; November 06, William Douglas McDowell, 32, shot; November 09, Anthony Lopez Lopez, 39, shot; and November 17, Antonio Frausturo Chavez, 30, shot. What about the list for the first half of the "Year of the Monkey", 1980: January 01, 1980, Benny Juan Martinez, shot, Dallas, Texas...January 06, Jose Vargas, killed, Dallas, Texas...February 27, Estela Salazar de la Cruz, 6, and Jose Anselmo Rodriguez, 55, shot, Laredo, Texas...March 27, Ja-Wan

# THROUGH BROWN EYES

Lydell McGee, shot, Baltimore, Maryland...the "Year of the Monkey" was still only half started.

# *THROUGH BROWN EYES*

## THEIR EDUCATION

Their Education Seems Meaningless

To Me, Yet,

Without Their Education, And Their Pieces

Of Paper.

I Cannot Find A Meaningful Job.

While They Are Taught

The Principles Of Progressiveness,

I Am Taught About Columbus.

While They Are Taught

The Positive Channels For Economic Advancement,

I Am Taught Printing.

And, While They Are Taught

The Very Meaning Of Their Existence

I Am Neglected Entirely Of Mine.

Their Education Is Meaningless To Me.

Yet,

Their Pieces Of Paper

Guarantee Me

Better Wages.

## I, CHICANO

I Am Chicano,

And I Will Always Be....

Chicano Till I Die,

For That's My Destiny.

I Am Of Mexican Descent,

And My Culture Is The Same....

My Language Is All Mixed Up,

But I Still Retain My Name.

I Am Honored To Be Chicano,

A People Great And Proud....

I'll Fight For What I Believe In,

I'll Repeat It Again, Clear And Loud.

I Am Chicano!!!

For That's

My

Destiny.

# *THROUGH BROWN EYES*

# THROUGH BROWN EYES

## Chapter 13

### THE YEAR OF THE MONKEY, Part II

July 12, 1980, found Flint, Michigan, in the middle of a riot. The outburst in the City of 16,000, which is 60 miles northwest of Detroit, flared Saturday night. The riot came after two Flint women (Black) were shot in the head, and investigators arrived on the scene. Tensions had been building since July 08, 1980, when a policeman shot a Black youth in the back.

Rebellion once again touched Miami, when policemen went to a housing project in Liberty City. Five Miami police officers were shot that first day of violence, and twenty-five persons were injured. The violence lasted four days, July 16, 17, 18, and I9.

Marvin Crenshaw, Chairman of the Coalition for a Citizen's Review Board, announced on July 16, that the Coalition would begin to raise petitions for a referendum on a Review Board. They had to raise approximately 38,000 names within 60 days.

Rebellion touched Chattanooga, Tennessee, too, on July 22, 1980. Blacks rebelled at an all-White jury's lenient verdict for three Ku Klux Klansmen who were involved in a shotgun attack on four Black women, April I9, 1980. They opened fire, reportedly, when a Klansman went "berserk" and started shooting when none of the Blacks seemed to pay attention to two crosses the Klan was burning in the Black district.

The violence erupted on July 23 and 24; 108 persons were arrested.

Regional Rebellion extended its arm to Orlando, Florida, on July 07, 1980, and lasted three days.

# THROUGH BROWN EYES

In Arizona, two ranchers get a mistrial in their case in which they "tortured and robbed three undocumented workers. This reinforces our opinion that the belief of justice for all is a false one.

More on justice. Dallas police officer, Danny Cain, 28, was no-billed in the killing of Samuel S. Stone on July 15, of this year, even though Cain lied three times in his report to the police on what happened.

Time ran out on the Coalition for a Citizen's Review Board. The group fell to raise enough signatures for a special election, on the creation of a Review Board, by September 22, 1980.

On October 10, 1980, according to a Dallas Morning News article, dated 10/11/80, Police officer Jerry Smith, 27, "was dispatched to Whitehall Laboratories, on a silent alarm call." He, allegedly, "was surprised by a man in a jogging suit who stepped from behind a dumpster and told him to freeze." Smith then turned around, screaming, and shot and killed Esteban Valderas, 21.

That would have been all to that story if the family had not called the Brown Berets. They were concerned about bruises they noticed in a picture shown to them by some officers who came to the deceased's family home to inform them of the killing.

An investigation by the Berets turned up information that implied that others might have been with Valderas, possibly witnessing the incident.

More importantly, pictures taken by the family clearly showed bruises about the face of Valderas, and a deep scar on his left leg, below the knee.

The Brown Berets turned over the findings to the Police Advisory Committee to add to the information received from the Internal Affairs Division in Dallas on that case on November 07, 1980.

The Valderas Family joined the Brown Berets, on December 14th, in attending a Police Advisory Committee meeting to introduce additional verbal information into the case.

21-year-old Armando Ayala and his friend, Ben Perez, decided to leave C. P. Wagner Park in Grand Prairie at about 8:30 p.m., on November l2, 1980. They noticed that a truck was following them.

Ayala asked his friend if he knew the people in the truck, and the friend said no. Ayala then got scared and sped off running two stop signs in doing so.

When they arrived at Ayala's house, Ben heard the driver of the truck say "I didn't want to shoot you." Ayala asked the unidentified man why he was chasing them. Just then a woman, who was with the driver, got off the truck and started arguing with Ayala. She yelled for him to come out and stop hiding under his mother's dress, and that he wasn't macho enough to come out.

Seven (7) police cars then arrived at the scene. When Ayala came to the door to explain what was happening, an officer yanked him out the house and handcuffed him.

While on his way to jail, Ayala said, he was trying tell Officer Reed what happened. Reed allegedly hit the recently discharged Marine, who wants "real bad to be a policeman."

The Dallas Brown Berets assisted Ayala in filling a complaint against the mistreatment on December 3, in Grand Prairie.

Remember the McDuffie case? Well, on November 10, 78, a former Dade County, Florida, Police Officer, Mark Meier, testified that he joined a cover up of the fatal beating of Black insurance salesman Arthur McDuffie, 33, on December 17, 1979, because of an unwritten code among officers not to "fink" on one another. "It's an unwritten law," Meier said, "an unwritten rule, a code of silence that you don't fink on fellow officers, especially when it's something of his own doing." His testimony was made during a trail for Charles Veverka, Jr., who got federal indictment for his alleged part in the murder. He was accused of four counts of conspiracy and being an accessory to the beating and cover up.

On the 23rd of November, 80, the Dallas Times Herald reported the following excerpts in an article titled "Police Face

# THROUGH BROWN EYES

Growing Number of Civil Damage Suits." "While public clamor for a Civilian Review Board of police brutality has mounted in recent years, an increasing number of attorneys have quietly sought another sort of Civilian Review of alleged wrong-doing by police officers- the review by 12 jurors in a civilian suit."

"I tell my clients that Internal Affairs is a waste time" said Attorney Dough Larson, who represented Washington (A Dallas citizen, who was the victim of police brutality, charged with assaulting officers, found innocent of the charges and won a $10,000 settlement from the City of Dallas for injuries). "By the time he (Claude Washington) was well enough to file a complaint, they said it was too late - which is a phony reason," he said.

The same article also included other cases which involved citizen legal-action against police:

"The case of Joe Donihoo and Keith Clasen. The city of Dallas agreed to pay the two men $25,000 and drop its appeal after a jury awarded them $54,000 in damages for injuries allegedly received in a 1977 police beating.

Donihoo and Clasen became involved in a scuffle with police when several officers were called to intervene in a dispute with a customer at Donihoo's used car lot.

The case of Marion L. Davison. Davison lost his sight in one eye when he got into a fight with an undercover Garland officer working in conjunction with Dallas police and Dallas Sheriff's officers at a Grand Prairie beer joint.

Davison negotiated a settlement of $15,000, of which the City of Dallas paid $6,500.

The case of Lee Douglas Page. He was fatally shot by Dallas police when fleeing an armed man who took him hostage as he left his South Dallas neighborhood for work last spring (1979). The City Council agreed to pay his wife and family $75,000 for his death.

The case of the Arlington woman, Mrs. Royden Sumblin, her daughter, Robbie, and sons, Ben and Rory. All of the Sumblins were injured in the July 1977 car collision, but Ben, then 8 years old, received the most devastating injuries. He suffered brain damage that diminished both his I. Q. and motor coordination, and injuries to his hearing and vision.

Attorneys for Mrs. Sumblin, Jack Pate and Boyd Waggoner, said she will receive either a $900,000 cash settlement from the City of Arlington, or annuity payments that will total more than $3 million over the years.

Incidentally, by the time you read this, we (the Dallas Brown Berets) will have submitted the following recommendations to the Dallas Police Department's Internal Affairs Division. We have very little faith that they will make any positive changes, but hope there is. Here are the recommendations in their entirety:

1. Extend the filing period to six (6) months, and for those who are hospitalized by the use of force by police, six months after the individual is released from the hospital.

2. The right to file complaints should be extended to the parents and/or guardians of individuals who are under 18 years of age.

3. The right to file complaints should be extended to persons who actually witnessed (either by sight or hearing) an incident.

4. The right to file complaints should be extended to the spouse of a complainant, when said complainant is unable to file.

5. Internal Affairs Division (I.A.D.) should accept any evidence alleging misconduct of an officer from any person, without filing a

complaint against the officer(s) unless the evidence is checked and found to be sustained, at time I. A. D. would file the complaint.

6. Conduct a "public awareness campaign" to inform citizens of the Internal Affairs Division, the complaint filing period and process, and location of main office and subdivisions.

On Thursday, December 18, '80, we found out that Dade County Policeman, Charles Veverka, was acquitted of all charges. "The atmosphere surrounding the trial was that they should pin a medal on Veverka since he was the only one who came out and admitted wrong doing." said John Sanders, Chairman of the Coalition Against Racism, which is composed of 30 community groups. "But the fact is that he did participate in at least falsifying records to cover up in the case of Mr. McDuffie. He admitted as much. He did lie; he did cover up."

A spokesman for the Miami Police Department told reporters that on December 17, after the decision, there were a "few isolated incidents, but no indication of anything major." But travelers were advised to "restrict their travel in areas where we experienced trouble in the past," and "some streets were barricaded."

"It comes as no surprise," John Due, of the N.A.A.C.P. said "to those of us who have watched the Criminal Justice System in operation. I think this trial plus the one in Tampa serve as indictments of our system of justice."

Black leader Marvin Dunn of Florida International University said, "I think the acquittals ought to be accepted for what they are- that the Criminal Justice System in these cases simply will not work."

Regional Rebellion lightly touched Miami again on December 18, '80, when several private cars and police cruisers were hit by rocks and bottles. On the 19th, Miami Police Spokesman, Calvin

# *THROUGH BROWN EYES*

Ross, said, "We are still getting reports of rocks and bottles being thrown at cars." Reports of gunshots brought at least 15 police patrol units with riot equipment swarming into the area.

And then, 200 people peacefully marched through Miami's rebellion-scarred Liberty City ghetto, on December 22, '80. The bi-racial Citizen's Coalition for Racial Justice said it wanted to memorialize McDuffie while protesting the acquittals of six (6) police officers charged with his death.

Citizens in Idabel, the scene of a smaller rebellion (than in Miami) in January, '80, responded calmly to the acquittal of a White man in the January shooting that killed a Black youth and touched off rioting.

More names for our list? YES!

1980 (part two):

January 01, Benny Juan Martinez, shot, Dallas, Texas... January 06, Jose Vargas, killed, Dallas, Texas... February 27, Estela Salazar De La Cruz, 6, Jose Anselmo Rodríguez, 55, shot, Laredo, Texas... March 27, Ja-Wan Lydell McGee, 17, shot, Baltimore, Maryland... June 25, David Medellin, shot, Euless, Texas... June 28, Fredrick William Paez, killed, Houston, Texas... October 10, Esteban Valderas, killed, Dallas, Texas... November 09, Anthony Lopez Lopez, shot, Dallas, Texas... November 11, Antonio Frausturo Chavez, shot, Dallas, Texas... Is this really the end?

CON SAFOS

## IT MUST HAPPEN

We Do Many Things Within The Movement,

Some Good, Some Bad,

But It Happens!

We Meet Many People Within The Movement,

Some Good, Some Bad

But It Happens!

We Accomplished Many Things For La Raza,

Some Good, Some Bad,

This Is Destiny

And As Always, It Must Happen.

# *THROUGH BROWN EYES*

---

## NO SOY SOLO

Yo Soy Un Representante

De Mi Santa Raza

Yo Soy Solo Una Vida
Que Se Muere Por La Causa

But I Will Not Die Alone

For There Are Many Like Me.

And When I Die...

"I Will Be One Less Chicano

Dying For The Cause"

Viva La Causa!

# THROUGH BROWN EYES

## IS IT EASY TO DIE?

Is It Easy To Die,

When All You Ever Wanted

Was To Live The Life

To Which You Were Born?

Is It Easy To Die?


Is It Easy To Die,

When The Person You Are Leaving

Behind, Is The Person You

Wanted To Be With For Eternity?

Is It Easy To Die?


Is It Easy To Die,

When You Know For Sure

That Death Can Bring Nothing

But Sadness Into The World?

Is It Easy To Die?


Is It Easy To Die,

When You Know That Someone

# *THROUGH BROWN EYES*

---

You Love Will Be Loved

By One Less Person In Their Life?

Is It Easy To Die?


Is It Easy To Die,

When All You've Ever Done

Is Only A Fraction Of All

That You Ever Wanted To Do?

Is It Easy To Die?


Is It Easy To Die,

When You Know That By Being

Alive You Can Bring More

Joy To Those Around You?

Is It Easy To Die?

# *THROUGH BROWN EYES*

## THE GOOD TIMES

One Of The Saddest Moments

Is The Death Of A Friend.

Like Losing Part Of History,

Which Was Always Close At Hand.

Whenever There Was Trouble

On Him I Could Depend.

Whenever He Needed Money

All I Could To Him I'd Lend.

We'd Sit Around And Talk About

The Good Times That We Had.

Sometimes He Didn't Tell The Truth

But His Stories Weren't So Bad.

Then There Were Times Of Sadness,

That Both Of Us Went Through

We Wondered Why Life Was So Bad,

The Life We Thought We Knew.

# THROUGH BROWN EYES

But Seldom Were The Fights,

When We Both Thought We Were Mad,

We'd Always Stop And Look At Each Other

The Best Friends That We Had.


Right Now I Feel So Lonely,

Right Now I Feel So Sad.

I Wish My Friend Was Here With Me

To Tell Of The Good Times That We Had.

# THROUGH BROWN EYES

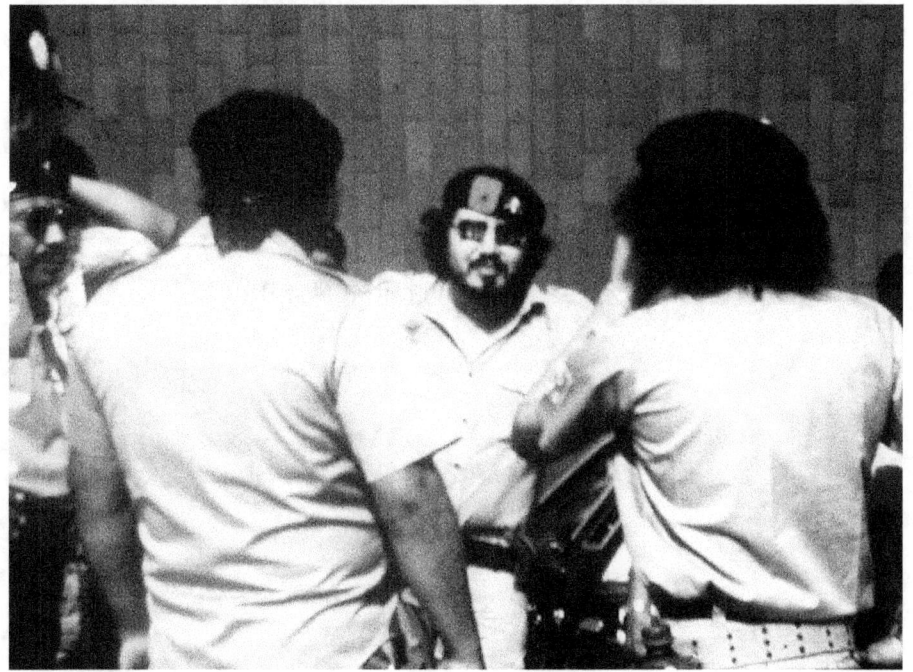

---

## **PEACE?**

What Is The Value Of Peace?

How Much Does It Cost?

When You Think Of All The Lives

That In Years Have Been Lost.

I Come To Think Of The Future,

How Someday It Must Be...

One Country Destroying Another

For A Peace Which Might Not Be.

To Kill Is A Crime So Bad

For Which We Make The Guilty Pay,

But In The Name Of Peace

We'd Let It Happen Every Day.

How Much Does It Cost?

What Is The Value Of Peace?

If We Don't Find The Answer Soon,

All Life On Earth In Its Name Might Cease.

---

# THROUGH BROWN EYES

# THROUGH BROWN EYES

## FINAL PALABRAS

First of all, in my capacity as the Public Relations Coordinator, I have had the fortune of being asked to speak at countless gatherings. Throughout all of the speaking engagements, I have been asked many questions. Most of these have been answered in the text of this book. In this chapter I will try to answer those questions that I feel have not been answered, as well as expound on any that I feel need clarification in more detail. I will take into consideration the fact that the reader cannot ask questions as I am trying to answer them.

One question that has continually surfaced is why the Brown Berets changed from a "community-service" group to a Nationalist Organization.

To be able to give the reader a good overview of the factors involved in this change we need to first understand the circumstances as they were and how the Berets reacted to them, as well as acted to them.

The Organization's name initially was the Young Christians for Community Action (YCCA). This group was organized by David Sanchez and Ralph Ramirez, with the help of a Catholic priest. The intentions of this group, to the best of my knowledge and resources, was to become involved in the community to try to better living conditions and the like. Other concerns included trying to get a better education for the youth of their community through trying to better the facilities and get better qualified teachers, etc.

After many attempts to resolve some of these concerns by going before city bodies, agencies, boards, councils, etc., the group decided that following the rules to the letter (such as going before the City Council and presenting a concern in the manner proscribed by law or ordinance ) was just not going to work.

The Organization then decided to become "more forceful" in their approach to the problems at hand. The "approach" that they chose was to change their name to Young Chicanos for Community Action (YCCA).

After realizing that changing their name was not going to bring about the effect they had hoped for, the Organization decided to try something different. Now, I am compelled to emphasize, at this point, that if following the "rules and laws" had worked, in the Organizations' effort to improve their community, they would still be the Young Christians for Community Action to this day.

But, as I have already pointed out, the system did not work for them.

The next step the Berets chose was to round up about a dozen members, get them dressed up in blue jeans, khaki shirts, and brown berets. Once they had this uniform on they started getting the attention of not only the City of "Nuestra Senora de Los Angeles," but also of the police and the news media.

After going awhile wearing this uniform, the YCCA became known as the Brown Berets. Many Raza preferred this name to the other because it was shorter.

# THROUGH BROWN EYES

The change that I am leading to came shortly after this. The Brown Berets, still working for "the betterment of the community," became more active and started developing much support.

The police, though, deserve much of the credit for the eventual change in the Brown Berets. They seem to have decided that the Berets had to be eliminated at all costs. The police started harassing and intimidating members very early in their development.

The Berets, on the other hand, started becomming concerned with why the police would be against any group that would try to better conditions in their own neighborhoods. Not knowing any reason for the attacks by the police, the Berets decided that in spite of all the problems that their community had to face, the police attacks on the Berets as well as many other Chicanos of East Los Angeles, was quickly taking priority.

# THROUGH BROWN EYES

It was not long after, that the main issue of the Berets changed from "bettering the community" to defending themselves and their community against the increasing police attacks on their people.

One would think that the police would realize what they were contributing to and change the tactics they were using. Nevertheless, they didn't. The police, instead, expanded their attacks. No longer was just plain harassment enough, the police started abusing, beating, and sometimes even killing the Chicanos who were so unfortunate as to be arrested by the police. Even, in some cases, when no crime was committed.

You must understand that even though all of this was happening to the Berets, most members still felt they could just bring all these injustices to the attention of higher authorities and that something would be done to alleviate the problem which was quickly growing out of proportion.

# *THROUGH BROWN EYES*

The real change in the Organization came after countless attempts by the group to resolve the problems by following required procedure (i.e. filing complaints with the Internal Affairs Division of the Police Department, filing complaints with the Justice Department, legal demonstrations, etc.).

Realizing that adhering to the law and "working within the system" would never work for them or other Chicanos, the Berets decided to work against the system that they had come to recognize as racist and impartial. They realized that the only way to make a system work for the people in general, and La Raza specifically, was to change the system. Thus the Berets decided that Nationalism (the act of being loyal and of being loyal and devoted to their own people; the sense of national consciousness exalting one nation above all others and placing primary emphasis on promotion of its culture and interests as opposed to those of other nations or supranational groups - Webster's Dictionary), was the only alternative. Another question that has come up frequently

is: What steps do the Berets take when deciding to become involved in issues and/or demonstrations?

Different Chapters have different methods of arriving at their decisions. In Tejas the Brown Berets already have procedures outlined in the By-laws of the State Organization which dictate which issues the group will take on and which issues the membership will avoid.

Once it is established that the Berets will work on an issue, a member, or group of members, will be instructed to review the matter and recommend any action, if any is called for. The membership then decides whether to take the steps recommended, make changes in the recommendations and implement them, or decide not to take on the issue entirely.

Preparing for a demonstration is one activity which requires much attention. Once the Berets have decided to conduct a demonstration, or even if they just happen to be providing security for another group's demonstration, the Brown Beret Security Force (BBSF) takes over. This section of the Berets is made up of some of the members who have shown interest, or have volunteered for, being involved in Security.

# THROUGH BROWN EYES

The job of the BBSF is to make sure that all will be in order before, during, and after the actual activity. In the Berets, when in a demonstration or other similar activity, the BBSF is in complete charge. The Minister of Defense, Security Minister, Security Director or whatever name the Organization gives her/him, is completely responsible for the outcome of the activity in reference to the safety of all who participate.

During the demonstrations, members of the Security Force carry walkie-talkies, canteens, and first aid kits. Members are usually in full uniform, which consists of combat boots, khaki pants and shirt, army belts, and in some cases, brown-colored army helmets.

Members are instructed to assume that the safety of the activity is already in danger and to actually prepare to defend the situation. BBSF members are trained to look for any problems or dangers which might exist. For instance, during a demonstration BBSF members are not only keeping the demonstration in order, but are watchful of any suspicious individuals as well as open windows in buildings cars, etc.

To what extent the Brown Berets will protect the demonstration depends on the extent of the danger that is imminent.

How do the Brown Berets select their officers? This has also been a much asked question. Again the answer is dependent on the locale of the Chapter and any local guidelines, but generally the decision is by consensus.

In Dallas, as in other Tejas Chapters, the decision for the top job comes in different ways. First, if a present Jefe (this is the name given to the appointed or elected leader of the group - pronounced "hefe") decides to abdicate his position, then the Organization either holds elections, or decides on a method of selecting an appointee for the position. On the other hand if a Jefe is found not to be applying his/herself to the philosophy and/or By-laws of the Brown Berets, or if the majority of the membership of that particular Chapter feel that a change in that position is necessary, then certain predetermined procedures are implemented.

The only way for a Jefe to be replaced except as in the first example above, is by coup d'tat (or overthrow of the existing Jefe and his/her followers) this can sometimes result in the expulsion of all or part of the "overthrown" members if they choose not to abide by the conditions of the "successors." And in times when a coup d'tat fails, the "rebels" are in danger of expulsion.

Should any reader have questions that I did not answer or points that I did not clarify, I will be exceptionally happy to receive correspondence on that matter.' I will answer all questions that do not violate the By-laws of the Los Brown Berets de Tejas, Aztlan.

Write to:

Brown Berets Organization
Dallas Chapter
P. O. Box 210763
Dallas, Texas 75211-0763
c/o Juan M. Perez, Public Relations Coordinator
*(NOTICE: the address no longer exists. For questions, go to: Chicanismos.com and leave me a comment)*

## THE DAWN OF THE REVOLUTION

Will There Be The Sound Of Rockets In Air,
Bullets And Bombs Producing A Scare.
Or Will We Be Voting To Make Sure And See
That Justice Is Equal For You And For Me.

The Day Of Deciding Is Getting Quite Near,
Of Living Together Or Living In Fear.
I Can Fight By Your Side, Against Our Foes,
Or Make You My Enemy And Give You Some Woes.

Together We'll Make This Country Real Strong,
To Fight Against Crime And Things That Are Wrong.
Apart We Will Cause It To Sway And To Fall,
Bringing Destruction To One And To All.

Listen To The Truth Of The Things That I Say,
As We Encounter The Challenges Of The Things That May.
To Destroy All Injustices, We Must Unite,
Or Else **_You_** Will Be In For A Hell Of A Fight!

**By Juan M. Pérez**

# THROUGH BROWN EYES

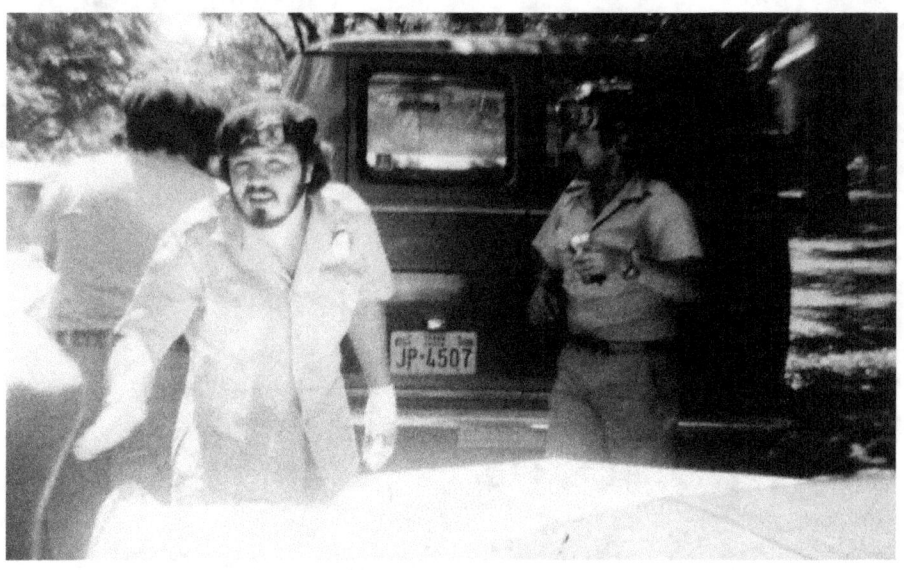

# *THROUGH BROWN EYES*

# THROUGH BROWN EYES

# *THROUGH BROWN EYES*

# THROUGH BROWN EYES

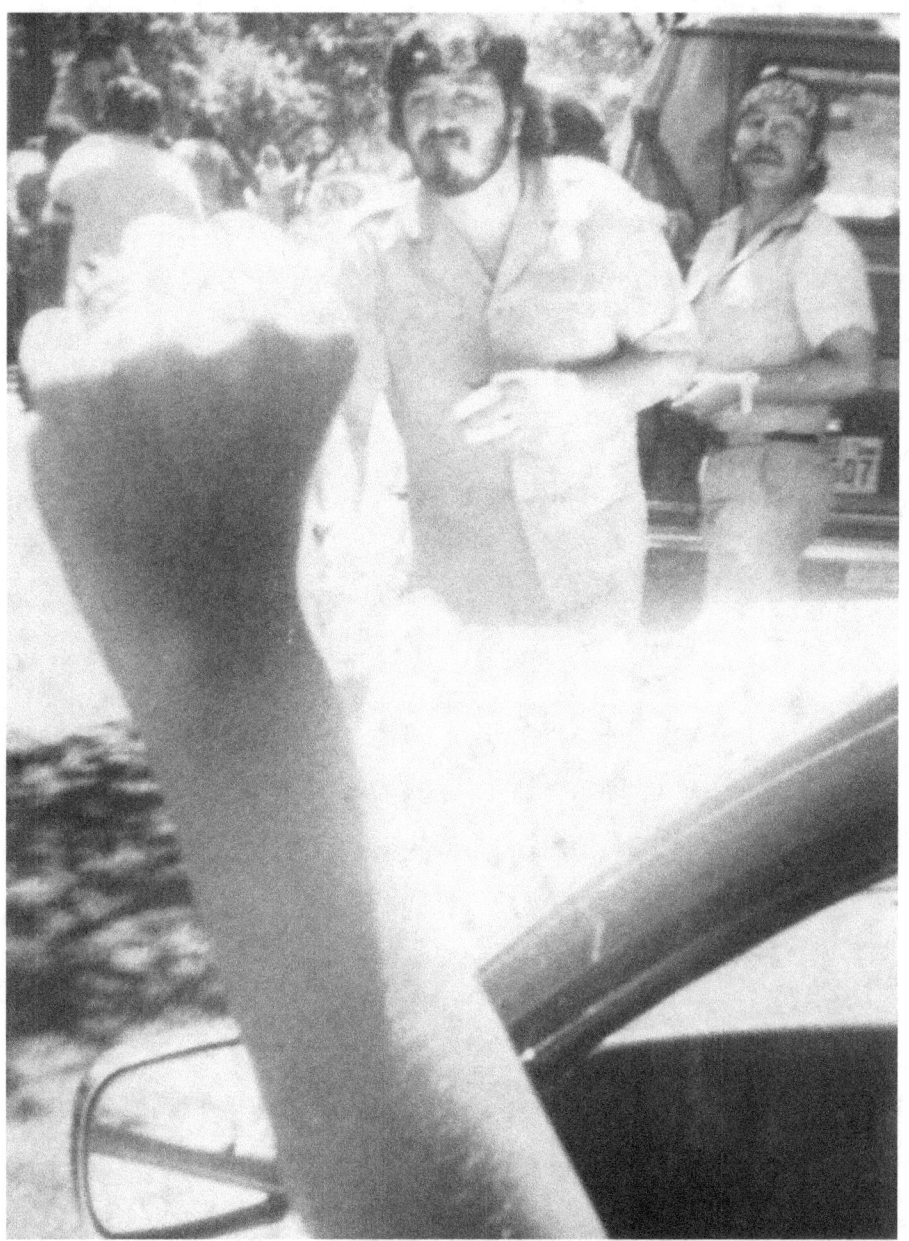

# THROUGH BROWN EYES

# THROUGH BROWN EYES

# THROUGH BROWN EYES

# *THROUGH BROWN EYES*

# *THROUGH BROWN EYES*

# *THROUGH BROWN EYES*

# *THROUGH BROWN EYES*

# THROUGH BROWN EYES

# *THROUGH BROWN EYES*

# *THROUGH BROWN EYES*

# *THROUGH BROWN EYES*

# THROUGH BROWN EYES

# *THROUGH BROWN EYES*

# *THROUGH BROWN EYES*

# *THROUGH BROWN EYES*

# *THROUGH BROWN EYES*

# *THROUGH BROWN EYES*

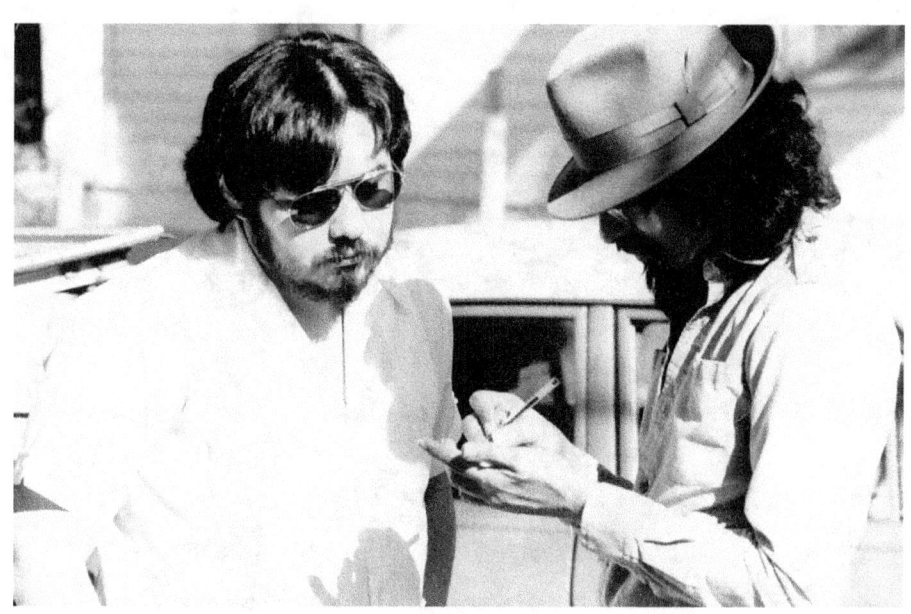

# THROUGH BROWN EYES

# THROUGH BROWN EYES

# *THROUGH BROWN EYES*

PERROS,
CHINOS
CISTAS

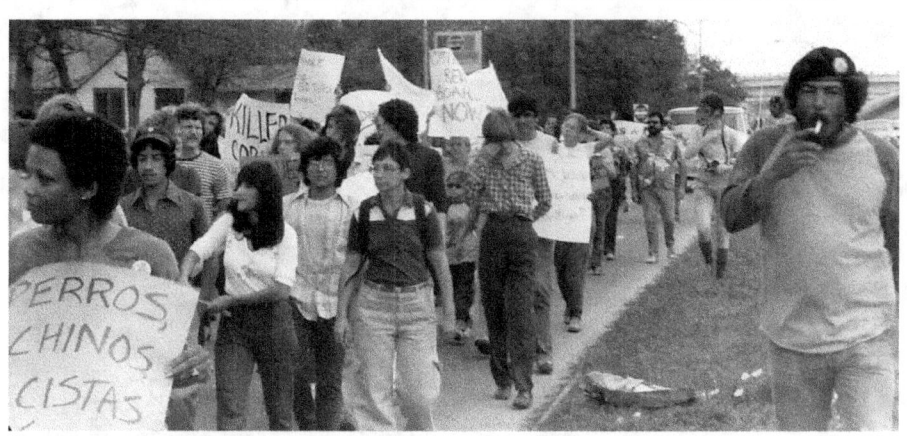

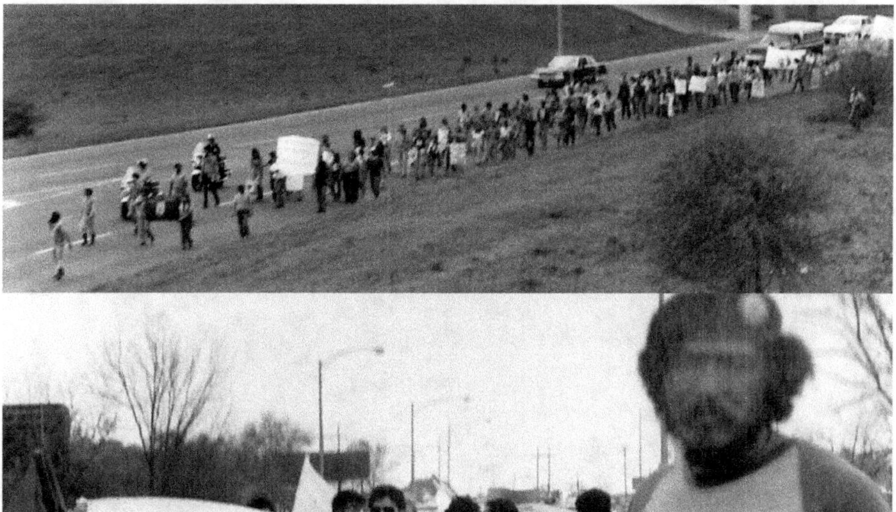

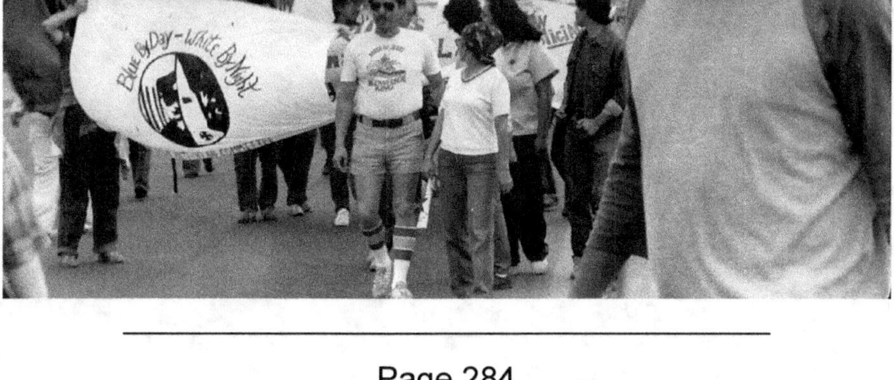
Blue By Day - White By Night

# *THROUGH BROWN EYES*

# THROUGH BROWN EYES

# *THROUGH BROWN EYES*

# THROUGH BROWN EYES

# *THROUGH BROWN EYES*

# THROUGH BROWN EYES

# *THROUGH BROWN EYES*

# *THROUGH BROWN EYES*

# *THROUGH BROWN EYES*

# *THROUGH BROWN EYES*

# THROUGH BROWN EYES

# *THROUGH BROWN EYES*

# THROUGH BROWN EYES

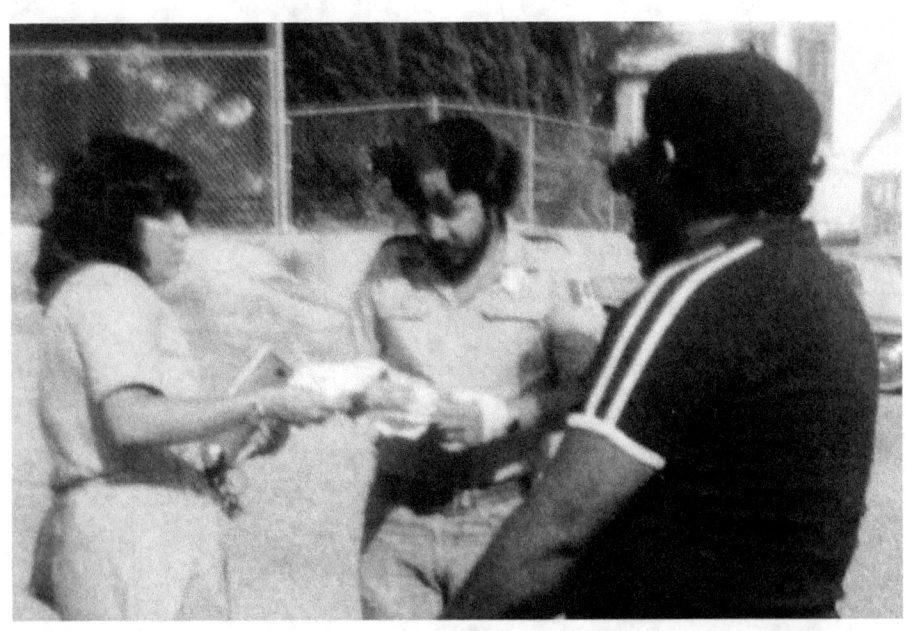

# *THROUGH BROWN EYES*

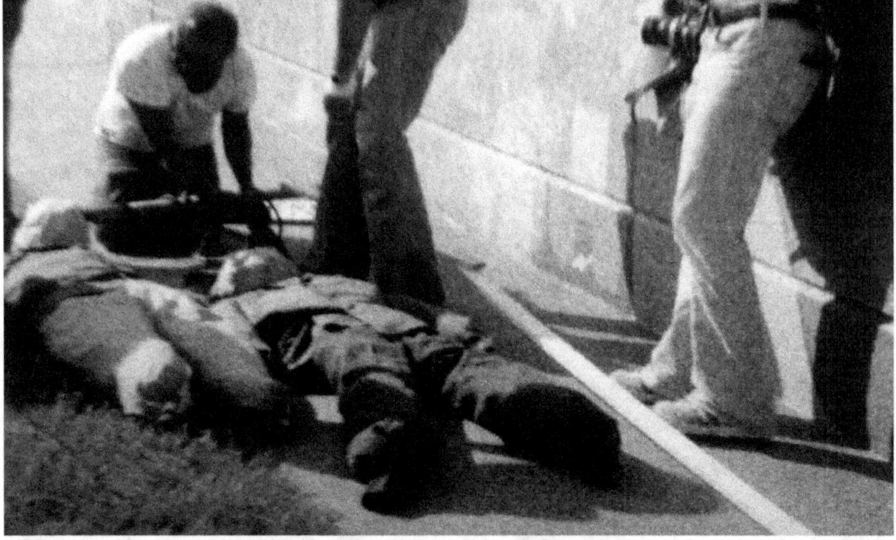

# *THROUGH BROWN EYES*

---

---

# THROUGH BROWN EYES

# THROUGH BROWN EYES

# *THROUGH BROWN EYES*

# *THROUGH BROWN EYES*

# *THROUGH BROWN EYES*

# *THROUGH BROWN EYES*

Staff photo by Jay Dickman

*Speaker uses bullhorn to be heard during rally*

# *THROUGH BROWN EYES*

# *THROUGH BROWN EYES*

# *THROUGH BROWN EYES*

# *THROUGH BROWN EYES*

# *THROUGH BROWN EYES*

# THROUGH BROWN EYES

# THROUGH BROWN EYES

# *THROUGH BROWN EYES*

# *THROUGH BROWN EYES*

# THROUGH BROWN EYES

A second book is in the planning which will include many more pictures. If you would like to be notified when it becomes available go to Chicanismos.Com and leave your email address.

www.ingramcontent.com/pod-product-compliance
Lightning Source LLC
Chambersburg PA
CBHW060235290526
45789CB00001B/51